The Cover Artist

MARIA SANDOVAL DE CASTAN

Maria Sandoval de Castan was born and raised in Cuernavaca Morelos, Mexico - a country rich in native creative arts. Her father, an architect, played a large role in her deep love and attachment to the arts and at an early aged Maria was often found exploring her artistic talents through arts and crafts, décor, and floral arrangement.

After marrying a culinary artist and Maître Cuisinier de France, Maria moved to Avignon, France where she fostered a great appreciation for Old Master's works and forged inspirational relationships with established French artists. Upon her return to the states, Maria and her husband settled in Laguna Niguel, California. There she decided to further her art studies, and enrolled in Saddleback College of Fine Arts. She focused on painting, drawing and even explored sculpture and ceramics. During her studies at Saddleback College she found her passion for portrait and figure painting with oil on canvas and pastel as her preferred medium. To further her new found passion for figure and portrait painting Maria spent some time in Chicago fine tuning her artistic style at the Art Institute and enrolling in courses at *Palette and Chisel* among many world renowned artists.

Maria continues to reside in Laguna Niguel, California but enjoys spending her summers in Provence, France and finds inspiration in French Artist's Atelier workshops. Currently, her works can be found in Cuernavaca, Mexico, at La Casona de Spencer Gallery.

FACING

the

HEAT

From my grand mother's kitchen
to working the line

Frederic C. Castan

Ed. Note: The successful life of a chef is normally depicted as someone who regularly steps out of the kitchen for endless curtain calls before cheering, well-heeled diners; earns glowing restaurant reviews; makes talk show appearances; publicity events; and receives eager reportage on new recipes—in short, one who lives a celebrity life.

The reality is quite different, however. Long hours, demanding and temperamental owners and managers, changing tastes, finicky customers, staff discord, harsh working conditions, restaurant closings, economic uncertainty, weekends and holidays spent away from family, the endless striving for culinary invention and perfection—all eventually exact their deep physical and emotional toll on an individual.

Frederic Castan, an award-winning celebrated chef who has worked at some of the best hotels in America as well as Hollywood's A-list restaurants, has seen it all. He has won competitions, been nationally recruited for prestigious venues, and has achieved membership in exclusive circles of international organizations. He's found joy and early success in a boyhood dream of becoming a chef, and he's known despair after placing his life savings into a new restaurant in Nice, only to be violently assaulted and his establishment trashed by the Corsican mafia. He has known poverty and exile in Mexico (and a wild restaurant shoot-out), family breakup, and the struggle to piece back a career. But he's never lost his boyhood love for the magic and joy of making meals for other people.

This is his story.

Facing the Heat

From my grand mother's kitchen to working the line

©2023 Frederic C. Castan

print ISBN: 979-8-35092-864-8
ebook ISBN: 979-8-35092-865-5

CONTENTS

Message to Aspiring Chefs

*O*n a flight from Chicago to Orange County, California, I sat next to a boy who was maybe seventeen or eighteen reading a food magazine and studying pictures of recipes and chefs. Intrigued, I asked him if he was interested in being a professional chef or just reading about the food. He told me, "I'm very interested in becoming a chef. I'm studying at the CIA in New York." CIA stands for Culinary Institute of America, one of the best schools of its kind in the United States. The tuition at that time, around 2003, was $22,000 to $25,000 a semester. It was very expensive.

I was curious. I asked him why he wanted to follow that path. He said that, for quite a while, he had been watching cooking shows on TV, many of which I knew nothing about. Once I watched *Hell's Kitchen* with Gordon Ramsey. The boy gave me some names, like Emeril Lagasse, Bobby Flay. He was fascinated by those shows and hoped one day to have that kind of career and host his own show. It was a powerful dream for a young kid, to be a celebrity chef.

I thought, *Wow! It's great to dream like that.* But to become a chef, it takes more than a dream. You have to be passionate about what goes into it. It requires a lot of dedication, a lot of sacrifice. When you are in school, it has a kind of pace. There's not a lot of pressure, no chef standing behind you all the time, criticizing you. Your holidays are free.

I told him about the conditions he'd be facing in the industry. "If you don't have the passion, if you don't like what you're doing when you go to work, if you can't work sixteen hours a day and not feel it, it's going to be very, very difficult," I told him. "You'll want to give up, because it's not what you were expecting to do.

"You've got to ask yourself, 'Do I really love what I'm doing? Do I have a passion for cooking?'"

He said, "Well, I like it. I'm learning."

Yeah, I thought, *but when you're not in school and you really need to go to work, it's certain that the day will come when you'll turn the lights out and wonder if you have what it takes.*

For example: the Sofitel, where I was working at the time, was new in Chicago. As executive chef, recently hired after a nationwide search, I helped make it a success. Our dining rooms were packed. Our brunch was so popular that long lines formed in the Chicago cold for people to get in. We got great write-ups in the papers and magazines. But I lived in a dreary little apartment where the bathroom door didn't close, and I had to fly to Orange County in California on my rare days off, because that's where my wife and family and house were and it wasn't practical for us to live together in Chicago.

This is only one of the many sacrifices you have to make.

The level of thought and struggle to maintain that effort never changes, from the first moment you put on an apron as a boy to the last time you take off your toque as a man advanced in years. And this doesn't include your management responsibilities. It's as hard as it ever was. It saddens me to realize what I put my wife and two boys through (most of the chefs I know are divorced). My body is exhausted more often now. I don't have a generous pension waiting for me. I have worries and anxieties most other professionals don't suffer in the autumn of their careers. Looking back, someone else in my shoes might wonder if I made the right choice.

Unlike most careers, the work doesn't get easier as one grows older. There's no hierarchy to rise through where you can delegate more responsibility to other people. You may have a staff of sous-chefs, chefs de partie, kitchen porters, and dishwashers to make sure a kitchen functions efficiently, but the requirements of purchasing, creating, cooking, and serving quality food, whether for restaurant patrons, hotel guests, banquets, wedding parties, religious occasions, pre-concert dinners, breakfast meetings, and luncheons, never change. People must eat, and even a short-order cook must feed them. As an executive chef, or chef de cuisine, you have to feed them in creative and fulfilling ways. You have to aim for what I call the wow factor.

That has been my lifetime effort and reward, and I wouldn't have it any other way.

In retrospect, there have been countless moments of pride: after my three teenage years of apprenticeship in Avignon in 1970, I received first place in my region in the French national EFAA (Examen de fin D'apprentissage Artisanal) competition. This is like a four-year completion in college. The contest is divided into four regions. I was from the southeast, the Provence region. There were twenty some students. You have to stand in front of a jury and cook from a basket of ingredients. From there you create your menu. After that you have to cook within three hours. A jury of eight then awards points. They look at cleanliness, how much you put in the trash—waste is another way to lose points—and then of course they judge originality, creativity, taste, look, and presentation—everything is about points awarded. And, of course, there's the time limit. You cannot go over the two-and-a-half or three hours; otherwise you lose points.

In the early years, I was awarded a plaque which reads, "This is to Attest that the Biography of Chef Frederic Castan Appears in the First Edition of the International Who's Who of Chefs, 2004[–]2005, Among the Greatest Chefs in the World."

In January of 2005, I was awarded "Association des Maître Cuisinier de France." The award was issued Par de President, Secretary-Generale. I was a member of the jury of Bocuse d'Or in 2005, in Chicago, for the selection of the American candidate to represent the US in Lyon, France, for the prestigious worldwide culinary contest Bocuse d'Or, founded by the world-famous chef Paul Bocuse.

Also, I was elected as a culinary advisor for the Confrérie de la Chaîne des Rotisseur; it's a worldwide association. A rotisseur is a chef from the period of the monarchy, who cooks poultry, wild game, lamb, and more on a rotisserie in the cheminee (fireplace). In 1952 the association was reborn to cook for high society that enjoys good food and wine and great companionship.

In 2006, I was inducted into the Academie Culinaire de France.

I was named chef of the year for Maître Cuisinier de France in June 2018.

I've never known any other life other than being a chef, beginning on June 28,1968, when I started at Hiely Lucullus, a two-star Michelin restaurant in Avignon. I remember that day well. I was aware of the war in Vietnam and political unrest in France. A lot of strikes were happening at this time. We couldn't get electricity sometimes for up to three days. There were no trains, no transportation whatsoever, no gasoline, no gas to cook on. The entire country was paralyzed.

When I told my mother about my life's ambition, she looked for the best restaurant for me to get work experience. At the time, there weren't many culinary schools in France. In Avignon we didn't have any at all. Andre Chaussy, my future brother-in-law, was already an accomplished chef. My mother went to him for advice. He said the best thing to do was to find work at a high-end restaurant and learn from scratch. Andre asked the owner of Hiely Lucullus if he could take me on as an apprentice. I was fifteen. There was no interview. My mom and I went to meet him, and he said okay. He called me "Petit," meaning kid, and said, "You will start Monday."

Hiely was the name of the chef-owner. It was a family-operated restaurant that opened in the late 1930s but gained its renown in the 1950s, earning its first Michelin star in 1956 and its second in the early 1960s. Its fame rested on regional spécialités such as terrine de foie gras aux truffes, pied et paquet (lamb feet and stripes provençale), brouillade aux truffes (scrambled eggs with winter truffles), les palourdes aux épinards, et les quenelles de brochet aux morilles, to name a few. Twice a day, an individual gratin dauphinois was prepared; it was the best in the entire region. Andre Hiely began training in the family restaurant (in Auberge) at a young age and went on to work with some of the best chefs in France at that time before he opened his own restaurant. He was passionate and strict. He never cut corners, was attentive to details in both the kitchen and the dining room, and was respected by all his guests.

Hiely Lucullus was the top restaurant in the region at the time. Mr. Heily named the restaurant after the Roman general Lucius Licinius Lucullus who enjoyed dining in luxury alone to appreciate and critique his servants' feasts. The restaurant was very elegant, located on the second floor with a beautiful view of the city, all white tablecloths, a lot of silver and crystal, and copper pans for the service done tableside.

My mom and I went to buy a uniform: a jacket and pants. I started the next Wednesday, June 28. (My brother-in-law later bought the restaurant, in 1993. It automatically lost one star when it changed ownership, but he earned it back.) I was scared. I didn't know anything. I said to myself, "My God, what am I going to do?" I was in the kitchen by myself. I worried about my uniform. I didn't know how to wear an apron, how to tie it. I needed to observe.

Every year, from mid-December to the end of February, the owner went to the truffles market every Friday and brought back 25 kgs of fresh truffles with mud around it—fresh from the soil. It was the apprentices' duty to brush them gently one by one, in lukewarm water, with a soft toothbrush. It took us almost a full day to do this tedious job. The truffle surface is very porous, you have to brush very delicately so as to not break it. Then we put them individually in a mason jar with an old Madeira wine and a pinch of salt, closed the lid, and put them to boil for about 25 minutes in order to preserve them for up to one to two years. We had truffles all year long, and what an aroma!

I followed one other apprentice, Roger, for a year. Everything he did, I had to duplicate. Every morning we had to wash five to 10 kilos of black mussels and a large bag of palourde (very tiny clams). I had to clean two cases of spinach after taking the stems out one by one and washing them two or three times in a big sink. When all those things were done, I gave them to another sous-chef to cook. Then I had to peel the potatoes and the carrots, with the chef continually yelling, "Come on, you've got to go faster." I cut myself a few time a week with the potato peeler and small knife. It was very stressful, but I always managed to do everything and go faster.

As the weeks went by, I started to help the other apprentices make ice cream, six flavors every day, fresh, twice a day, morning and night. We had an old ice cream machine with a ball that went around in water, which we called the saumure. It's a bath of minus twenty-five degrees, salted so that it doesn't freeze. The ball went around inside the salted bath with a motor on top and a big harm going into the ball to mix the ice cream; the machine would turn, like a mixer, if you will.

We did three or four quarts every day of each flavor and put them in a pot that went into the freezer. We didn't have an ice machine; instead, we had a big metal rectangular tank maybe three feet long and six inches high and eight inches wide, which we filled with water and left overnight in the salted water bath where the ice cream machine was, to make ice. In the morning when we arrived, before we made the ice cream, we put the tank under the water so that we could remove the ice from it and break it for ice cubes, the wine buckets, or glasses.

On the first day, when I had to remove the tank from the saumure, I took it by bare hand and held it. It was probably a good forty pounds. I had to go maybe ten feet to the sink. My hands stuck on the metal. Oh my God! I don't know how many degree burns I suffered on my fingertips. I couldn't touch anything for weeks. I was in pain. Cold is harder to stand than heat.

I cried.

But those were good lessons in the beginning, cutting myself, burning my fingers.

The ice cream was kept in a large freezer box called an ice chest. We stored the dinner plates there. One morning, I was carrying six or eight dinner plates to put in the ice chest. I was about seventeen at the time. I'm 5'10" now. I was maybe 5'6" then. To reach the bottom of the chest was hard for me. And there was the weight of the plates. Maybe I was slow; I don't know. The chef got a little pissed off, saying, "This guy's so slow." I was hanging over the side of the chest, and all of a sudden, he kicked me in the ass and I fell in with all the plates. He called me "petit con," meaning stupid. I don't know how many broken plates I had to throw away. I had to throw away ice cream too because broken pieces of the plates got mixed in.

That was a terrible day.

During the first few months, things typically happened like that. It was a tough experience. Every week one of us apprentices would have to cook for the staff, including nine in the kitchen, two dishwashers, nine servers, the bartender, the chef, and the cleaning lady. We served twenty-two people. Every day, morning and night, that was the job of the apprentice. They'd tell you each day what to prepare.

The first day I was in charge of dinner, I was scared that I wouldn't be able to do it. I had to do good because Mr. Hiely and his son Pierre were eating, too. He was strict. We cooked anything from steak to fish to stew. Sometimes I had only twenty minutes or a half hour to cook it. Quick, quick, quick! I had to be ready by eleven o'clock because everybody was already seated. By eleven forty-five, everyone was up and off to work again. My job was just to cook. The cleaning lady brought her food to the table. I didn't eat with the others. I had the first course and second course, and that was the way it was done.

I learned a lot. Week after week after week, after six, seven, or eight months, you start to work with the other chefs for the guests. So, in the morning was the ice cream duty, then the cleaning of mussels and spinach and other vegetables, then putting stuff away and cleaning and so on, helping the dishwasher sometimes, and then cleaning the kitchen, stove, and floor, cleaning everything, including shining the copper pots.

That was my basic duty as an apprentice for the first three or four months. Slowly I began to do more and more. After eight months, I began to work as an associate with the chef to do all the grilled stuff. One day, Mr. Hiely, who was seventy-two, and Pierre, who was about forty-five, started yelling at each other so loudly that they had to close the restaurant. Everyone went home at six o'clock that night. That tells you how temperamental those people were.

A story to share . . .

Few weeks after I started my apprenticeship, the chef asked me for the blue paint for a dish we had on the menu "Truite au Bleu" (blue trout). I didn't know anything about that blue paint and asked the chef where the paint was. He answered that the paint was finished and to go ask for it at a nearby restaurant. Of course, he was needed as soon as possible, so here I was running in Avignon's street looking for the famous blue paint. I stopped by the first restaurant, asked the chef for the paint, didn't have any, and sent me to another restaurant. I started to be very worried not to find the paint, so I went to three different restaurants, running very fast, with no luck. Finally I went back to Hiely Lucullus, empty hand, no paint to be found. I was afraid to be yelled at, but when I told the chef I didn't find it anywhere, everyone started to laugh. For a minute I was wondering why. Well, it was a big joke—it is not such a thing of blue paint! The trout became blue just after being killed. It is dropped in vinegar, then becomes blue right away.

Inheritance from My Dad

The restaurant was literally 1,000 feet from the home where I grew up. I was born October 14, 1952, in Avignon, a small city nestled on the Rhone River. It's surrounded by a stone wall built during the Roman Empire, and there's a big castle located there. In the 14th century, Pope Clement V moved from Rome to Avignon where the papacy remained for over 70 years. Avignon has a famous bridge, the Saint Benezet, named after one of the popes but also known as Pont d'Avignon. It was cut in half during a flood in 1669 and never repaired. Today, as the capital of Provence, the city is a big tourist destination famous for its summer art festival. There is also a nearby vineyard called Château Neuf du Pape whose wine enjoys world recognition.

The city today is very different from the city I knew growing up. I lived in a working-class neighborhood on Rue des Teinturier (dye textile factory). It was post-WWII in character. Our house was built during the 1850s and was three stories tall. There I lived there with my father, mother, and my sister, Genevieve, who is five years older.

My father was an only child. His dad died during the First World War in 1914 when my father was only three months old. His name was Frederic, just like mine. He was in an army cavalry unit called the tirailleur, fighting in North Africa. That's where he died, in Oran, in Algeria. My father's name was Georges.

My father had a very hard life. His mother died when he was at a young age, as well; I think he was only ten or twelve. He not only had to survive, he had to feed his grandmother. It was not an easy life, especially during the war. There were shortages. The weather was bad. There were a couple of years of freezing temperatures and floods from the Rhone. It was just him and my great-grandmother living in the house. He didn't go to school. He barely knew how to write and read. He worked as a stonemason, cutting marble for cemetery headstones. He smoked all his life, very strong cigarettes, Gauloises.

That was his youth.

At the age of 18, he joined the French railroad. He moved up the ranks until his job came to be in-charge of an entire train. You have the conductors, and then you have the person responsible for the operation of the train. Whether there's a derailment, or it arrives early or late, the director must remain aboard at all times. But he never worked a set schedule. I remember instances when he went to bed, and a few hours later, in the middle of the night, an agent from the railroad company would ring the doorbell to deliver an order for a new assignment to board a train, sometimes for as soon as within two hours. Sometimes he rode up to ten hours at a time. He'd pack a bag for his lunch or dinner consisting of a sandwich, cheeses, and always some wine.

I never heard him complain. He was a very hard worker. On his off time, he did handyman work: wallpapering, painting, plumbing, and electrical repair. He liked to help others, including neighbors and friends.

He never refused a request.

"Hey Mister Castan, can you help me do the wallpaper?" Yeah, boom.

Those were not his only activities. There was a monastery in Avignon where many Carmelite sisters lived. They had a big garden, three or four acres in size, and grew all kinds of vegetables and fruits for the nuns, in addition to a small hospital of maybe 25 rooms. He took care of the entire garden, worked the trains, and did all that other work. He was rarely home.

My dad felt compassion for my mother's parents. He helped them in their farm whenever necessary.

He was my role model; I learned many things from him, including helping on the farm.

In 1939, a freight train he was working on was seized by the German army and diverted into Germany. He was taken prisoner; the war had not even started yet. He was one of the first to become a prisoner. In a few weeks, the second world war was declared.

At first, he was a prisoner on a farm, then they transferred him to a camp, not a concentration camp, just a camp. He was there for two-and-a-half years. After that, in 1942, the prisoners were sent to Siberia. They were forced to walk outside in below-zero temperatures to the point where my father had his fingertips and feet taken with frostbite. All his life he suffered from that. Every time the weather got cold, his fingertips would break wide open. It's a terrible thing to have to endure. His feet were deformed to where it was difficult for him to wear shoes for the rest of his life.

I remember the day my mom cooked a liver at home for lunch and he became hysterical over the smell. He lost his temper and blew up at my mom. The reason for his outburst was the memory of the camp and what happened there. I was probably eleven or twelve. He was really enraged. Later, I asked him why. He said that, when he was in Siberia, they used horses to do a lot of the work. When one of them dropped from exhaustion or cold and lay dying on the ground, the men ripped open the stomach and grabbed its liver, still warm, to eat raw. It was an act of survival. My father couldn't stand it. That smell at lunch brought everything back to him. Oof, it was bad.

Sometimes he had cramps in his leg where he couldn't move. That would make him very upset; he would lay down on the floor. That was when he grew temperamental. He'd throw things.

We didn't have a refrigerator at this time. We didn't buy one until I was ten or twelve. We had it only a week before he got so mad because of the pain in his feet that he punched a dent on top of the refrigerator. The mark remained there forever. We couldn't remove it. One time he angrily pushed the dinner table with such force that all the plates flew off it. He frightened me. But these actions came from what he endured from his youth on, with no parents, no siblings, and then the war, being a prisoner for over five years, plus the horror he saw during that time. All these things had a big psychological impact on him. Sometimes it would make my mom cry.

But besides that, he was a very loving person. He was thoughtful toward us, bringing home the best things he could find in the market. He'd bring us fruits and vegetables from the garden. He was very strong, very fit. He didn't go to the gym, but he bicycled and gardened for four, six hours at a time. He walked. He was always doing something. I never saw him rest any day of the week.

He had a friend who lived on the French Riviera. The only access to his villa was stairs. There were probably 70 or 80 steps going down. There was no road above. You had to take those stairs. On one occasion my father helped him fix his house and carried big cement bags of 50 kilos on his shoulders. They were 120 pounds each. He carried them down the stairs, up the stairs, back and forth, more than 50 bags, one by one. I tried to lift one. It was impossible.

He helped my grandparents on the farm. My grandfather on my mother's side had grape vines, so my father helped make wine as well, crushing the grapes, supervising the fermentation, filling the sixty-liter barrels, and leaving them for four to five months. Then he put them in the bottles, so we'd have about 400 bottles of wine.

My father was raised Catholic. He liked to be surrounded by friends from church, and from those, he made us help out at school at fundraisers. He knew everyone in the city.

Sometimes, while he was gardening for the nuns, a messenger from the railroad company would arrive at the house and say, "I need him to work the train at four in the afternoon, or one o'clock in the afternoon."

My mom would go to my dad at the convent and say, "He's here," and my dad would say, "Alright." Then he'd come home and take a shower. We didn't have a telephone. We had no other way to communicate with the outside world. We didn't have a car. We didn't have a TV. We didn't have anything at the time. The first TV we bought was in 1969. I was raised with no TV and a big, big radio.

We rarely talked about the war. It's something he didn't like to bring up. But it did leave scars. He'd come to my bed before I went to sleep to give me a kiss goodnight. I could sometimes hear the radio in the middle of the night as he got ready for work. Then he'd walk down the stairs and go off on his bicycle in the dark and cold night.

My family and I last saw him in 1982 when we closed the Pancho Villa, a Mexican restaurant I'd opened in Nice the year before and gave up for a number of reasons that were beyond my control. He had helped us decorate it, and now he came to help us close it. I took him back to the train station in Nice with my two kids and said goodbye, knowing it would be the last time we'd see him. I knew I wouldn't be able to come back to France for quite a few years. I didn't think he was going to die, but it was difficult. He was heartbroken to see us go, especially the kids, because he didn't have a chance to really enjoy them. He died of bone cancer in 1986.

A Mother's Love

My mother was a truly compassionate woman. I remember once when a beggar knocked at the door, she opened it. The guy had an old empty can. She filled it with soup and gave him a piece of bread. She'd often take me on her lap, and I would nestle my head in her chest, listening to her singing songs or telling me a short story.

She passed away in 1978 after a difficult and painful battle of liver cancer that lasted about six months.

My mother's name was Josephine. She was born in 1919 and raised on a farm in Barbentane, which is about ten miles from Avignon, across a small river called the Durance. My grandfather also lived on the farm. She was born number five of six kids and grew to become a petite woman, around 5'4". She had a happy childhood, but it was hard working on a farm at a young age. Money was minimal. When the war started, and the Germans occupied France. They came to the farm and took everything they could find, livestock, produce, wine, anything to feed their troops. They left almost nothing for my mother's family. It was a tough time.

She married my dad after the war, in 1946. By that time, he was one of the last prisoners to be released. Most of the guys from the village were prisoners who came back in late '44. mid- '45. Everyone thought he was dead. But when he did return, he married my mother in May of '46. I don't think he knew her before that, but Barbentane was a small village, ten miles from Avignon. They may have known about each other. He was first released in

Germany. I don't know how he got home. If it were now, I know we could talk more about his imprisonment in Germany and about his hard labor in Siberia. But he didn't like to talk about the war, especially to a little kid. Then I left home at an early age, so we really didn't have time.

She was devoted to the Catholic church and helped raise money for the church and the schools all year long. She did all this walking because there were no cars, just bicycles. She was dedicated to helping people, including the lonely. There was an older lady who lived by herself on the same street. My mother would visit to see her, sometimes buy groceries for her, sometimes just keeping her company and doing a little cleaning. Besides that, twice a week she visited my grandparents on her bicycle, 15 km away, sometimes with me on the back, to do house cleaning and prepare meals. My grandmother had become too asthmatic for housework. My mother would do the cleaning and laundry by hand because there was no washing machine and no water from the city. The water came from the ground. You had to pump it by hand. There was no refrigerator, no bathroom, no shower, or anything like that. To take a bath, you need to heat water on the stove, pour it in a big zinc drum and take it standing up.

That was a tough time. At the end of the day, we'd ride home on the bicycle, ten miles one way. Avignon was a windy city. Sometimes the trip was very difficult. The mistral (a famously destructive wind that sweeps through the Rhone valley) comes through there. It can gust up to a hundred and forty kilometers an hour. It's almost like a hurricane. Chimneys fly away. One time I saw a tree land on a roof.

She lost an eye in the late 60s—she had a tumor and they had to remove it—and couldn't see well after that. But she raised two children, my sister and I, while doing house cleaning and preparing lunch and dinner every day and helping in the church. She was a very busy woman.

She and my father were happy together, except for the days when he'd lose his temper. She was a very loving mum, loved by everyone in return. When I was a boy, she liked me to lie on her lap for a long time, caressing me. Once in a while on Sundays, she'd invite dozens of ladies from church to share coffee and cake and spend all afternoon talking about different things.

One day when I was ten or twelve, I told her, "I want to make the cake today." At first she refused, but I insisted. I followed a cookbook recipe and made the cake! That wasn't the only reason that I later wanted to be a chef, but my instinct for it was already there, and I liked that the more I worked on the cake, the more I enjoyed it. When I put it in the oven, I had to watch closely to make sure it didn't burn because the oven didn't have a thermostat. It was a charcoal oven, so it could get too hot or too cold. It was tricky. But after twenty-five minutes, the cake came up alright. I took it out and cooled it. I didn't know how to make butter cream, so I just took some butter and chocolate and kind of whipped them around. The cake had no filling inside, but that was it, basically.

The ladies enjoyed it. My mom served tea and coffee with it, so after working from late in the morning to five in the afternoon, it was very rewarding that I could bake a cake that came out so well.

I spent a lot of time watching my mom cook, but from an early age, I also spent a lot of time on the farm, helping out all summer long. I watched my grandmother cook while my mom was in Avignon. She was a very good cook. Watching her was a good experience in learning how to taste.

On the farm, the main summer crop was tomatoes. We harvested about three thousand pounds every other day. Some were too ripe; some were cracked. We couldn't bring the bad ones to market, so we put them aside for my grandmother to use as preserves.

It was very interesting to watch her make preserved tomatoes.

First, she removed the top of the tomato with a knife and made an incision on the bottom. Then she put it in a large pot with boiling water, let them boil for a few seconds, and removed the skin. Then she cut the larger tomatoes in half, removed the seeds and put them in a mason jar, and pressed them down. She would make a puree with a pressed puree out of the smaller ones and put it directly in bottles with a special cap to make a preserve. They were sterilized in water in a huge pot over the wood fire in the chimney outside for about an hour and a half. We had tomatoes all year long. What a delight!

She processed apricot and peach preserves the same way, pears as well. I was fascinated to watch my grandmother cook, puree, and then peel and cut vegetables for dinner.

My uncle Louis was fanatical about bullfighting. Once in a while, he took me to see one as a treat. They were staged in the old Roman arenas in surrounding cities like Arles and Nimes. It was a little scary for me as a boy to see one, but nevertheless it was kind of fun.

After the fight, a bull's remains went to a butcherie next door to the arena, where they sold the meat. He'd buy two or three pounds. The meat was very dark, with no fat. We'd take it home for my grandmother to make into a stew, called Boeuf a la Camarguaise. You can't get this in America. It's from Camargue, the region in southern France where the bulls live in their wild state and where the guardians—the cowboys, if you will— pick them up on horseback for the fights.

I can describe the recipe. The beef was marinated in red wine, vegetables, and aromatic herbs for the night and then quickly seared and cooked in the same red wine with onions, capers, pickles, tomatoes, thyme, garlic, and parsley for a good three to four hours, very slowly, in a wood stove over charcoal, in a very heavy pot.

She prepared it in the morning, and we had it at night for dinner. I still remember the taste. The beef melted in your mouth. We ate it with white rice from Camargue.

All those dishes had a huge impact on me, the ways they were prepared, the time they took. It basically took all morning to make that dish from the night before. Because Boeuf a la Camarguaise is a dish you could eat two to three days in a row, we were able to enjoy it that night and the next day and the day after. So from that time, watching my grandmother and then my mama cook was like watching a seed flourish.

In Avignon, at the age of thirteen, I went to different places to watch chefs cook. I went to one place called Hotel d'Europe. There was a little alley behind the restaurant. The windows were open. You could hear everything that went on in that kitchen, the pots and pans, the loud voices. You could feel the atmosphere in the kitchen. My imagination was working. I stopped in the alley for maybe three or four minutes, just to listen. If you like planes, you go to the airport to see and hear what goes on. The same with trains. I was very attracted to the kitchen like it was a movie set.

I was at the door where the delivery guys got in with all the produce, sea food, meat, and poultry. So I followed and could see part of the kitchen and what's going on: a guy cutting, another guy sautéing, to see not what they were doing because I didn't know what they were doing, but just to see the action and the uniforms, the chef's hat, all of them cooking together, me thinking, *I want to be there"* It was a combination of things that attracted me to that kitchen, that profession.

After music lessons, I watched chefs in their kitchens, cooking. I felt the excitement, saw the synchronization to get to the final dish. I was probably fourteen or fifteen. Later, when I started my apprenticeship, I became intrigued by well-known chefs. I asked my mom to buy me books so I could explore the lives of chefs like Picard. Another one was Paul Bocuse. There was a famous hotel in the south of France called the Hotel Baumaniere. Picard was the chef there. Bocuse was a three-star Michelin chef at a restaurant in Lyon, called Paul Bocuse. Another guy was Roger Verger. This guy had his own hotel and restaurant above Nice. Another one was Trois Gros, two brothers who were well-known chefs. They worked in Roanne. Another one was Alain Chapelle. Another was Michel Guerard.

I was intrigued to learn about them, looking at pictures and reading about what they were doing.

I didn't have too many friends. There was school and there was music, and I didn't have time for friends. My vacation was spent on the farm, working with my grandfather, my grandmother, and my uncle. Friends didn't exist for me. There were a few at school, but when I started to work, no more. Friends became people I worked with—other cooks.

So I read these books with the hope that one day I'd become one and work with one of the great chefs. I learned about their discipline and preparation. Most of them started around my age, 14, 15, even younger. Most of them started directly in small shops as apprentices. They didn't go to school. Some started in big restaurants where chefs took them under their wings.

I didn't talk to my parents much about these people. They wouldn't have known who they were. But for me, particularly when I started to work, I'd talk to the chefs. It was like talking about painting to a master like van Gogh. You want to know more. You look at the painting and want to know how he did it, how he put it together. I read about one artist who painted three or four pictures a week. It's amazing. They never stop painting for ten, twelve, maybe twenty hours. That was their life.

So I was inspired to keep pushing my limit. That was my message—to be inspired. You read books and magazines, you get inspired by other artists, other masters, other chefs. You see what your style could be. If you look at Asian chefs and ask yourself, "Do you want to be like an Asian chef?", you say, "No, it's not my style." You go with the chef who has the style that you like.

My style is in my blood. It's where I'm coming from, which for me is the south of France, Provence to be exact, with a Mediterranean flavor, using products from the region like olive oil, fresh herbs, garlic, and all variety of seasonal fresh vegetables and fruits from the farms; everything there had so much taste and flavor.

This is what I like to do. Keep pushing your limit and think outside the box. meaning, For example, what can I do with that tomato if I can cut inside to make a tomato salad? Can I do something else, like with a stuffing? And then combine with something else? You can definitely do other things.

The tomato was one of the main things we cultivated in summer, so I am familiar with the taste of just picking from the farm. In my career, I've tried some and didn't know what I was eating. There's a big difference between a tomato that's just been freshly picked and a tomato that's ripened in a box for three or four weeks and has no taste when you eat it. When you go in the field and touch a leaf, and the smell comes directly to your nose, and you say, "Wow!"

My mother was very energetic, always moving, walking to the supermarket. Actually, we didn't have a supermarket at the time. We had a butcherie, dairy store, bakery, and fish store, and we went from one store to the other. We never had to buy produce because my dad bought it from the garden of the nuns.

We had huge family reunions, especially on Christmas and Easter. There were up to twenty-eight who came to our home, including my cousins, uncles, and aunts. She had six brothers and sisters, some of them married with kids. My mom welcomed them all, making a big lunch, doing the dishes, and preparing for dinner again. She'd prepare a salad with a vegetable called cardon. It's like a celery, white and bitter; you eat mainly the hearts, with anchovies and a garlic dressing.

She would serve escargots. My father collected them throughout the year, put them in a cage for months to empty their stomachs, and he'd add some fresh thyme to flavor them a little bit. Then, for dinner, my mother would soak them in salt water so that a membrane that was formed over the opening of the escargots would break. They'd seem dead, but after fifteen or twenty minutes, they'd wake up and try to climb out of the pot. She had to put on a lid or they'd climb up the wall in the kitchen. When they did, she caught them and put them back in the pot. She'd wash them a couple of times. Then she prepared a court bouillon: water with carrots, onions, celery, leeks, garlic, and herbs. She'd cook them for thirty or forty minutes and then take them out of the pot, then make Armoricaine, a sauce based on garlic, onions, ripe tomatoes, spices, and cognac. She'd finish with some of the court bouillon from the escargots, and when the sauce was done, she'd cook it all up, and that was the meal for the entire family. While doing this, she cooked leg of lamb and roast chicken from the farm. This was a typical dish while she also made ratatouille: a stew with zucchini, eggplant, tomatoes, bell peppers, onions, garlic, and fresh herbs, slowly cooked in the oven for over an hour. She also cooked other vegetables for dinner.

For Christmas every year, escargot was the main dish. Then we had thirteen desserts, which is typical for Provence. When I say thirteen, almonds could be a dessert, grapes another. One of them was the Yule log made by a baker friend of my mom. There was a true wood log in it. The baker took the log, nice and round, about three inches in diameter, and wrapped a biscuit around it, with cream in between, and then decorated the top with different Christmas ornaments.

Every year we had at least one newcomer in the family. It could be a cousin bringing a girlfriend or a new wife, or maybe a new neighbor—always someone new for dinner. And that person would cut the cake for dessert. That was a tradition. We give the knife to the new person. So imagine a girl of eighteen or nineteen years old; she doesn't know anyone in the family yet. We give her a knife and say, "Okay, you cut the cake." She starts, and when she gets to the wood, you can see her face. She's thinking, *What's going on?* After a few seconds, everybody starts to laugh. Then of course we tell her what it is. That was the kind of fun we had for years. We drank wine, cracked jokes.

After that we went to the midnight mass. Mass was beautiful. It went back two or three hundred years. All the shepherds appeared to make a carriage full of flowers, produce, fruit, and accompanied by sheep. The first would be the one with the horns—the rams. Then you have the sheep, real animals pulling the carriage into the church, and shepherds both in front and behind with a lamb over their shoulders. All the women, carrying gifts, wore costumes in period dress from the time of the Nativity. Then there were the parishioners. The church was completely filled up. You couldn't get in. And it was always cold. The mass would last until one thirty or two in the morning, with the choir and everyone else singing.

After that, we went home and had more food. We ate a bread called fougasse. It's a dough with pieces of pork inside, like bacon, dry and crisp, made with olive oil. They also put olives in it. We also had dry fruits, chocolate, and coffee. This was at two in the morning. Then we'd open gifts, because Santa Claus had come while we were in church. We'd go to bed at three thirty, maybe five, in the morning. I believed in Santa Claus for so long that it never occurred to me to ask who stayed back to lay out the gifts. It was a very innocent time.

So that was the holidays when we had all the cousins and family around big tables. My sister Genevieve and I helped do the dishes. She was like my dad, big-hearted but not as much involved with others. She was much more sentimental than me. She married at nineteen, when I was fourteen, and lived close to my mom for the first couple of years. When she had her baby, my mom helped her a lot.

But we were not close growing up. The age difference was too great. When she was dating, I was still very young. Then she married and had kids and her life with her husband.

They're still married. He was my first chef and mentor. He was the chef at the first restaurant where I went to work.

Soon after they got married, I started my apprenticeship with her husband at the same restaurant where her husband was chef de cuisine. They lived right next door to my parents' house, in a small apartment. After work, late at night, we all get together in my mother's home in the kitchen. My mom always prepared something to munch on with tea or hot chocolate. We could spend a couple of hours chatting about many different things, how can I improve in my work or simply some joke that my mom came up with.

We did this for a while until my sister had her first child Isabelle. She insisted that I will be her Godfather—what a joy when she announced it to me. And to that day, we are still close together. My sister worried many times about me. Even though the distance and communication are not the best, but she has always thought and cared about me and my family.

MA MAMAN ESCARGOT A L'ARMORICAINE

Serves 4

Escargot Ingredients

4 dz. of escargot in the shell
(that hibernate for 6 months)

1 carrot

1 rib of celery

1 onion

1 small bunch of thyme

3 bay leaves

4 ea. garlic cloves

Pinch of salt

First let the escargot soaked in salted water overnight, then wash them very well under runny water. Prepare a court bouillon in a sauce pot with 2 quarts of water over high heat. Add all vegetables cut in large pieces, herbs, salt. Let simmer for 10 minutes, then add the escargot, bring back to a boil, and remove it from the heat. Let the escargot in the court bouillon until cool down. Then strain them ,discard all vegetables. Reserve it on the side along with the court bouillon.

ESCARGOT SAUCE ARMORICAINE

2 shallots chopped fine

4 garlic cloves chopped fine

1 tablespoon of tomato paste

4 ea. ripe tomato (skin less, seed less) diced

2 cups of dry white wine

1 cup of brandy

1 bunch of thyme

2 bay leaves

1 quart of the court bouillon from the escargot

1 pinch of Espelette pepper (basque chili)

½ cup of olive oil

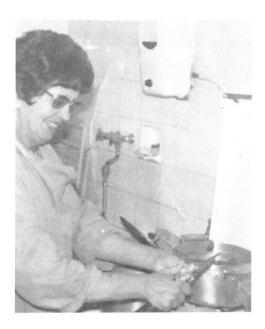

Preparation

In a sauce pan with olive oil, over medium heat, sauteed shallots, garlic, add tomato paste, then add diced fresh tomato. Saute for a few minutes. Add thyme and bay leaves, then add the escargots gently so as not to break the shell. With a wood spatula, mix them well into the tomato preparation. Add the brandy, ignite with a long match or lighter, and while it flambees, add the white wine. Let it reduce by half. Add the court bouillon, Espelette pepper, and a pinch of salt. Let simmer for about 30 minutes with a lid on. Serve 12 escargots per plate. Add some sauce. You should have a small pick to remove the escargot from the shell.

Bonne degustation!

Summer's Inspiration

We took our annual vacation at the end of June every year for three weeks on the French Riviera, in Roque Brune Cap Martin, to be exact, next to Monaco. Roque Brune is the name of the village. It's only three miles from Monaco. Since my dad worked the train, we didn't have to pay for the ride. At four in the morning, we'd walk all the way to the train station, about a mile and a half, with big suitcases. As a kid, I was really scared. My father packed huge boxes of vegetables from the convent's garden, including fruits, whatever he could put in, to ship ahead of us and enjoy while on vacation.

My father had a good friend who had been a prisoner with him during the war. He had a big family in Cap Martin. They were wealthy and had a little house with two rooms, a kitchen, and bedroom with a terrace that was part of their big house. They let us have it for free. In exchange, my father helped them fix stuff. Since we had a big kitchen, he'd bring the edibles we'd eat outside on the terrace because it was always warm out there. And we all slept in the same big bedroom, which had three beds, one for my parents and one for us. We were only a quarter of a mile from the ocean and the beach, easy walking distance. A train ran between the beach and the house.

To get to the beach, we had to walk down maybe fifty to seventy stairs. That was a big, big treat. We spent ten hours at the beach, from nine o'clock in the morning, a quick break for lunch, and back until seven at night, when it got dark. We'd play with rocks because there was no sand. There weren't many other kids. We played with my dad who spent time with us when he wasn't working on the house. My ma liked to spend time with us on the beach when she wasn't cooking or cleaning.

Twice a week we'd have to leave at six in the morning to take the train to Monaco and shop for food. I loved to see the market with its meats and the fish fresh from the ocean, the produce too, because my dad never brought enough to last us for the whole three weeks. It was fascinating, so I always wanted to go with my mom to help with the bags. It was a great time for me to go through those big markets with their beautiful smells. Once a week, my mom was making a dish, Barbajuan, a specialty from the region. They are kind of fried raviolis with a stuffing made of green chard. This was a treat for me, because I was helping her and they were so good.

There were days when my dad took me to the beach to look for crabs. We'd bring them home, and I would help my mom make a seafood soup. First we would saute the onions, celery, fennel, carrots, and garlic. Add fresh tomato, add the live crabs and some herbs, and finish it with white wine.

After spending time in the Riviera, my family took the train four hours from the Mediterranean to my grandmother's farm in Barbentane, near Avignon. It was the center of my existence, basically. Between school and the music conservatory, Barbentane was where my youth was spent, beside my annual three-week vacation.

When my grandmother cooked stew, I remember to this day how she did it every step of the way. This, for me, became a passion. I could stand all day watching.

Life was wonderful; I had no complaints. Fish, produce, cheeses, meat, fruits—I was excited to see all those things even if vacation lasted only for three weeks or less. I was five or six years old when we first went, and I kept going all the way up to age fifteen, every year, from June and the end of school, through July. Then, when vacation was over, my family stayed on my grandmother's farm for two months and a half to work all the rest of the summer.

BARBAJUAN RECIPE

Serves 6

Ingredients for the dough

11 oz. of ap flour

1 whole egg

2 oz. of extra virgin olive oil

7 oz. of water

Salt

Ingredients for the stuffing

1 lb of green chard

2 whole eggs (beaten)

4 oz. of white rice (cooked al dente)

5 oz. of parmesan cheese (grated)

2 oz. of ricotta cheese

1 onion chopped fine

2 garlic cloves chopped fine

Canola oil for frying

PREPARE

For the dough, mix flour, egg, and olive oil in a bowl. Add the water slowly and keep mixing. Once the dough is done, knead the dough on a table, make a ball, cover it, and refrigerate it for a few hours.

For the stuffing, cook in boiling water the green chard. Once tender, transfer it to an ice bath, then pat them dry. Cook the rice in water until al dente. Strain it. In a skillet with olive oil, sauteed diced onions, garlic until translucent. Add the green chard, then add rice. Sauteed this for just a couple of minutes. Transfer it in a mixing bowl. When cold, add eggs, both cheeses, seasoned it, and set aside.

Take the dough and cut small pieces at a time. With a rolling pin, make the dough thin (like a lasagne), and with a round food cutter, make a circle. Put some stuffing in the center, brush the edges with some beaten eggs, fold over like an empanada.

In a large skillet with oil (½ inches), over high heat, fry those empanadas on both sides until golden. Then put them in the oven for 10 minutes at 350 degrees.

Eat it when warm during cocktail hour.

The Good Catholic Boy

We lived inside the ramparts that surrounded Avignon. It was often windy. The mistral drove people crazy. It ripped tiles from roofs. It uprooted trees. It could blow as much as 80 miles an hour and come anytime, summer or winter. But Avignon is a big tourist stop, particularly in the summer. It eventually outgrew its walls, but the traditional city is inside, along with the cathedral and five or six other churches. When I was growing up there, the population was sixty-five thousand. Now it's about a hundred thousand. There are big mountains that surround it, up to fifty-five hundred feet high. Nearby Mont Ventoux looks like the moon on top. It has no trees or grass.

The big activity is the month-long Avignon Arts Festival, which was started in the early '50s. I've been only once. There's dancing, opera, ballet, and theater. It draws people from all over Europe and the United States. It takes place in different historic buildings. Ballet and music are performed in the Palace of the Pope.

More on the mistral, which is an important part of life in Avignon. It begins in the Alps and follows the Rhone River. It can also bring heat in summer, up to ninety degrees. When it gets to Lyon, it becomes really strong, because there's a big valley that allows it to gain strength. After it hits Avignon, it travels to Arles and into what they call the delta. It can last as long as a week.

I rode my bike to school in all kinds of weather, cold, hot, windy, whatever. The first school I went to was St Jean Baptiste de la Salle. It was a Catholic school. I didn't like it much from the beginning on. Once, when I was about twelve, we were sitting in a classroom, and the teacher, a monk, was pretty strict. It was cold outside. There was a lot of fog on the window, which was near my desk. While he was teaching the class mathematics, I got bored, so I started to draw a bicycle on the window: the frame, the saddle, the handlebars, the wheels. I did every detail. The teacher watched me but didn't say anything. He let me draw for twenty minutes, one hour, and when I finished, he came up, grabbed my ear, and said, "I need two hundred and twenty like this tomorrow morning." So I had to draw two hundred and twenty bicycles, exactly the same. My ma and I stayed up until two in the morning making the drawings, twenty or thirty bicycles a page. I was about twelve.

I don't know why I didn't care for school. I didn't like to sit for a long time, first of all. We had those desks that opened up from the top. I'd open mine and put my hand in, and the teacher would come along and slam the lid on my hand. It was stuff like this that made school unattractive to me. That's why when I went away for summer vacation, the school would give me a lesson book, maybe twenty-five pages long, in French and mathematics, for me to do a couple pages a day. I'd wait for the whole summer to go by, and then at the end do it all at once, because I didn't like it. I didn't like reading books.

At night I went to the conservatory of music to learn violin and the French horn. I played them for seven years, from age seven to fourteen. I started with the violin, but my teacher told my mother that I'd never be great at it so I should take a brass instrument. I wanted to try the trumpet, but there was no more room in that class, so that teacher recommended the French horn. There were only three other students. So I took French horn for about four years. Once I gave it up, I never played again. I like classical music—my wife loves it—but I'm not a big enthusiast. I like to go to concerts now and then, but I'm not that involved in it. My sister, on the other hand, played piano for many years.

I was thirteen when I announced to my mom that I wanted to become a chef one day. I got into that more and more after watching my grandmother make preserves and work the farm all summer long with all those animals and other stuff. It was through seeing all her love and passion for what she was doing, and the time she took to do it, and in helping her, that it came to me: *Wow, this is what I want to do.* I touched the food.

My ma taught me also by example. When I was home through ages twelve, thirteen and fourteen, I helped peel vegetables and whatever else she was doing, like making beignet, a zucchini dish that is a specialty in Southern France. She then made a nice tomato sauce using my grandmother's tomato preserve. This was a whole meal on its own and delicious.

Years of helping and watching her is why I decided to become a cook. When I told her of my decision, she said, "Are you crazy? You have to work weekends. You have to work holidays. You work late in the evenings. When your buddies ask if you want to go out for dinner or to the discotheque, you won't be able to go with them. You'll be like a slave in the kitchen, working long hours where it's always hot." I mean, she put me through so many things to discourage me from doing it.

"No, you should become an engineer on the train. Your father could help you. You could go to school for a couple of years, blah blah blah."

"I don't care!"

I talked to her so much about it that she couldn't object anymore.

Finally, she said, "Okay. You want to become a cook, be a cook. But remember something: Once you've started, I don't want you to come back to me after a few months, six months or a year, to tell me it's too hard, it's too whatever, and you want to switch to something else. You're going to stick there, and that's it. Understand me."

I said, "Yeah, Mom," and that was it.

After that, she looked for the best place for me to go. There were no cooking schools in Avignon. She went to my future brother-in-law, Andre Chaussy, for advice. He said that the best thing I should do is go to a high-end restaurant, to learn from scratch. Then she asked if he could make a space for me where he was working. He was a very good chef. So he arranged for the restaurant owner to take me on as an apprentice. There was no interview. My mom and I went to meet the owner, and he said, "Okay, you will start Monday."

The name of the restaurant was Hiely Lucullus. I started there June 28, 1968. I was fifteen.

MOTHER'S ZUCCHINI BEIGNET RECIPE

Serves 4

Ingredients

3 medium size green zucchini	Some beer
4 oz. of AP flour	Regular olive oil
2 whole eggs	Salt
½ cup of milk	

Prepare

In a mixing bowl, whisk eggs and flour. Slowly add the milk, and add the beer. The consistency needs to be like a cream. Sliced zucchini about ⅛ of an inch thick, and add it to the batter. Put oil in a large skillet over medium heat. With a slotted spoon, take some zucchini wrapped in the batter and drop it delicately in the hot oil. When golden, flip it on the other side, (cook it for 2 more minutes), then remove it from oil and set it over a paper towel to pat them dry. Season it with salt and pepper. If you desire, you can put over a light tomato sauce.

Hiely Lucullus:
Lessons from the Kitchen

*T*hings happened at Hiely Lucullus that were not a lot of fun.

One day my buddy Roger was making a dish called pieds et paque, a specialty from Provence. It's made with lamb's feet and the paquets are made with tripe. He couldn't see well and wore very thick eyeglasses. That dish is very gelatinous because of the lamb's feet, and the sauce is thick. Along with tripe, a piece of the stomach, you make a package which consists of stuffing made with parsley, onion, garlic, and a couple of other things. You make a package and tie it up with a butcher string. Then you put it in a pot with all the feet, the condiments, chicken broth, tomato, and white wine and cook it for a good six to eight hours in the oven at a low temperature. Then, when it cools off, the bones are removed from the feet, but you don't remove the string because everything will fall apart.

When an order comes to the kitchen, you take three packages and a piece of the feet, and with the sauce you heat them up. Before you send them to the guest, you remove the string, put the little packages in a clay pot along with the lamb feet, drain the sauce over, and add some parmesan cheese. Then you send it to the guest.

One day we were very busy, behind, and running fast. That kid was just one year older than me. He was making that dish on order and transferring the sauce to the crock pot. But before that, each of the strings had to be removed before straining the sauce. While doing that, the steam came up and fogged his glasses so that he couldn't see. He removed the first two strings one, but the third one he couldn't see. He took and put it in a dish with the feet on it. The boss was behind him, watching everything. He saw that the string was still on. No one told Roger, "Hey, watch the string." So the boss waited for him to finish everything, pour the sauce over, and take the crock pot, which had handles on both sides to put it on a tray for the server to take to the guests. While he was doing that, the boss got so pissed that he threw the crock pot, filled with hot gelatinous sauce, in his face. The kid had to be rushed to the hospital, screaming. His face was badly burned.

There was another time that made me wonder about my decision to work as a chef. There was a regular customer in-house who always ordered the same dish, Fricassée de Volaille au Curry. We were taught to cook the chicken on the bone at the order. Once cooked, we trimmed the bones that stick out from each piece, finished the sauce to dress the chicken, and then sent it out with the waitress to serve from a copper pan tableside. I was falling behind, and when the chef called for the Fricasse to be sent to the guest, I moved the chicken forward without trimming the bones sticking out. I quickly added the sauce and then pushed it out. Five minutes later, Mr. Hiely came back to the kitchen with an angry expression. He yelled, "Who is the stupid that sent the chicken this way without trimming the bones?" Everyone in the kitchen got very quiet, looking at each other. The head chef looked at me as he knew that I was the one that did it. He motioned his head towards me as if to say, "Are you going to confess or what?" So I didn't have any choice. I said, "It is me!" As soon as I said it, I saw an 11-inch round China plate with remnants of chicken dinner coming toward my face. I just had the time to duct under the table, and the plate flew above my head.

From that day on, I never cut corners.

Cooking requires the use of all the senses. There's touch, a feeling that goes through your fingers, a distinct sensation about the product quality, ripeness, density, and fluffiness. Touch conveys meaning. There is also the visual. You can see if a fish is fresh or if the meat looks fatty or not. The odor is also very important, not only to differentiate the fragrances between plants and herbs, but also the freshness of a fish, poultry, and more.

Another sense that comes into play in the kitchen is sound. You can hear if a steak or chicken breast is searing or steaming because the heat is too low under the pan or if it is boiling too fast for a chicken or fish stock.

Sometimes I'll position myself where the server stands to pick up the plates so that I can see the other cooks. I can watch the guy on the grill cooking the steak. He may forget it while he's doing something else and I can see that the steak is getting burned on one side. I'll yell, "fleap the meat! It's getting burned! It's getting overcooked." There's no such thing as undercooking meat on one side and overcooking it on the other. You have to cook it evenly. The timing is something you have to learn after many tries.

You can't go by a clock or watch. How long it will take to cook a roast or a whole chicken is not an exact science. It all depends on the type of oven, and the temperature, so the best way is by watching closely and touching the meat or poultry. Using a thermometer to make sure it is done right is a good method now.

But I learned and learned well, to the point where when I was ready to do my examinations. I took two: one called EFAA, for when you work for a restaurant owner, and the other for when you go to school, called the "Certificate Aptitude Professionnel." You have to take cooking tests and written tests for both. All these certifications take place three years after working in a restaurant, like going to college. You serve an apprenticeship, and then you become a professional.

For the EFAA, the owner as sponsor must state, "I am the owner and this applicant works for me." That's what the owner of Hiely Lucullus did. I wanted to do the CAP as well. And he told me no, because I hadn't gone to school to prepare for it. "You will not be able to do it." That's what he told me. He was scared because he was responsible for me and did not want to have a bad reputation in case I failed.

So I said, "Okay, I'll do it on my own. I won't put your name anywhere." So I didn't. "If I don't pass, you don't have to worry about it."

During the summer of 1970, I was a guest of the students of the school in Marseilles. I was about eighteen. All students from that school got a recipe book to study over the course of three years in order to be ready for the final exam. Since I didn't attend that school, I never received that book to study. I said, "Who cares? If I don't pass it, I don't pass it."

I went in for the test. They gave me a menu. Everybody has a different menu so that you cannot copy information. For that, you have to list what you need from the market. They give you fifteen minutes to figure out what and how much you need for each ingredient for each dish you had to do. If you forget something, it's tough luck.

I gave my list to a member of the jury. He went and got it for me.

That's what I did. They also judge you on your market list. For me, it was already something I did every day. But for the students it was more difficult to fill in three hours; they lacked practice. One of the students spent so much time doing roses with potatoes, and using red food coloring for it, which bled onto his uniform, that I don't think he could finish his dish. I kept my focus on organizing the sequence of the three dishes with just the right amount of ingredients. Once the budding chefs chose their menu, they were tasked the responsibility of calculating the right amount of ingredients for the recipes to feed four judges.

The menu was simple. The first course was vichyssoise, a leek and potato soup, served cold. The main dish was chicken Normande, consisting of a mushroom cream sauce over a bed of rice and garnished with seasonal vegetables. The final dish, dessert, was a layered sponge cake with chiboust (pronounced chi-boost) and creme anglaise. Chiboust has the consistency of pastry cream mixed with whip cream—it's light and thick—whereas the anglaise cream is saucy.

We had three hours to complete a three-course meal. I finished in two and a half hours, during which I almost lost my cool when the oven kept shorting out while my sponge cake was baking. I found out later that the hairdresser's drying machine next door was on the same circuit, and every time the hairdresser turned it on, the circuit would break. But I managed to bake a beautiful sponge cake. Afterward, I looked for a judge to make him aware I had finished. When I found one, he couldn't believe that I was done.

He said, "Are you quitting?"

"No, I'm finished."

"Already? Well, okay. If you have everything ready, put your three dishes on the table for the judge to check, and please make two plates of the same dish. When you're finished, you can go home."

I dressed up my three dishes twice, one for the jury to taste and one for the photo. I cleaned my station and left.

I waited about 10 days and went back to see the result. Guess what? I came out in first place. I won regional first place for the CAP and the second place for the EFAA competition too. I was very proud of myself and went to see the boss and said, "I got first place."

"Wow, good job."

So now, technically, I am a professional. I deserved to be paid for working. But Mr. Hiely did not want to pay me while I was still under contract as an apprentice for another year. So the only way I could break my contract was to ask permission from the Ministere des Armees to go early to do my mandatory military service in France. The normal age to go to the service is 19, and I was barely eighteen. Three months after my demand, I was called to leave and join the French Navy.

GRATIN DAUPHINOIS HIELY LUCULLUS

Serves 4

Ingredients

2 large Idaho potato	1 cup of milk
5 oz. of grade gruyere cheese	Salt
1 large garlic clove	Pepper
3 oz. of butter	

Preparation

Take a shallow ovenproof dish about 10 inches diameter and 1½ inches deep. Butter the bottom of the dish with your finger. Puree the garlic clove and spread it all over the dish. Peel the potatoes, and slice them thin (like potato chips) with a Mandoline. Right away, before the potato turns black, lay a couple of layers of potato chips and have them flat and evenly spread. Sprinkle a bit of salt and pepper, cover with milk, just above the potato, cover it with cheese and a few drops of butter. Put them in the oven at 350 for about 20–25 minutes. The gratin should be nice and golden brown.

The French Navy

*O*n 1971, I was drafted into the Navy where I worked as a cook on a destroyer for one year. I believe the law in France changed in the late seventies, but until then, every man who was physically able had to do military service for 14 months. The Vietnam War was coming to an end.

I trained for eight weeks in a big camp next to Bordeaux, at Lake Hourtin, along with three thousand other recruits. The training was tough. I was skinny and small. They made fun of and bullied me. I was maybe 5'8". Compared to the other recruits, rugby players who were 6'2", 6'3", and maybe 240 lbs, I was at most 140 lbs. Once while marching, one of the guys in the back put his arm between my legs and lifted me up high.

One day, I did something wrong. I forgot what the infraction was, so instead of putting me in jail for a few days, they sent me to a big pig farm next to the camp. Three thousand pigs! All the guys like me who were being punished had to clean out trash from the camp, which included separating the cans and glass from the food. Once you did that, you put it in a drum to feed the pigs. So I had to feed 3,000 thousand pigs. When they smell food, they charge you. They were in slots, maybe ten pigs to a slot. My job was to put food in there, and my God, it was not funny. I was scared. They made a lot of noise. It was terrible.

I was assigned to a ship, a destroyer "Duperret," which was already gone from the port when I was deployed; it was anchored a couple of miles off the coast in Toulon. I had to take a landing craft to get to it. As soon as I boarded, I began to feel dizzy and nauseous. They put me to work right away with eighteen or so other cooks. The kitchen was just above the engine, so the floor was hot, probably as much as a hundred and twenty degrees. My legs grew numb from standing up. The ceiling over the kitchen was very low. You had to walk with your head down. The chef's way of cooking, particularly chicken, was very poor, and the presentation very sloppy. I was disgusted.

There were two 40-gallon tilt brazier pans. My higher-ranking superiors told me they were going to make pasta and that I needed to fill one of them up. So I filled it, closed the lid, and turned on the thermostat to boil water and cook the pasta. After a while I saw water steaming over the side. I opened the lid. The pan was full of hundreds of cockroaches floating over the water. We were on a time limit and the chef insisted we keep on, so I removed the roaches with a skimmer and cooked the pasta in the same water.

Nobody got sick.

Before I got on the ship, they gave me a huge immunization injection. For two days after, I couldn't eat anything besides chicken broth. My shoulder was yellow from the size of the injection. That was an experience.

When we finished cooking, I took a break for a couple of hours between shifts and went to lay down on my banette (bunk bed) with my chef's tunic still on. Since my legs were numbed from the heat, I did not feel roaches on my legs, but as soon as my legs got cold, I felt the roaches crawling all over my legs. All I could do was shake them off. We weren't allowed to complain.

That ship, built in 1948 shortly after World War II, was eventually decommissioned and rebuilt as a nuclear destroyer.

There was a big sonar unit in its stern. It was the only ship of its kind in the French Navy to have sonar that reached as far as it did. In one instance, we had fifteen or twenty civilian engineers come on board for an inspection tour. The ship's commander, for whom I always made special dinners, said that those engineers were going to dine with me in my quarters so I should make a nice meal. We always kept good stuff in the freezer. We prepared lobster, made like my mother would make, Armoricaine (I remembered my mom when she did the escargot with the same sauce for Christmas).

So I started to cook.

We had a huge coffee percolator that could make 60 gallons of coffee. It was like six or seven feet high, filled at the top with coffee grounds.

The speakerphone warned us to expect high winds within the hour, winds as strong as the mistral. I knew I had to be ready for a rough sea. But I didn't know that the ship would suddenly begin a sharp turning maneuver. All my lobsters flew off the stove into the wall, spraying my sauce all over. Cans rolled along the floor, back and forth, and coffee grounds flew all over the kitchen. This went on for a good fifteen minutes. The floor grew slippery. I opened the door and stepped outside. I saw all the civilians puking over the rail.

The commander called to cancel lunch, which was great because it was already on the floor. And as I was ranked a matelot, the lowest class seaman on the ship, I was the one who had to clean it all up.

On another occasion, everyone was given condoms before we went ashore in North Africa, specifically Abidjan on the Ivory Coast. That was basically the only experience outside France I had. All the sailors just blew them up as balloons, threw them away, and went into town to get laid anyway while the condoms lay floating around the ship. I didn't go. They needed someone to stay on board to feed the other sailors who stayed behind.

A month after that, the ship went to Brest in Brittany to be decommissioned and converted to a nuclear destroyer. We were part of a group of eight or ten ships that had to go through Gibraltar between Spain and Morocco. A month before that, there had been a bad accident in the same place. A French destroyer, Surcouf, had been badly damaged after a collision with a Russian icebreaker and then broke in half after the French attempted to tow it. I think everyone was drunk on the French ship. Nobody was on the bridge, and the vessel was on automatic pilot. Nobody checked the radar. The destroyer was on a path that put it in front of the icebreaker. When they found out and sounded the alarm, it was too late. The ship couldn't stop. Six sailors died, including two bakers who were cooking bread—this happened at one or two in the morning—two or three mechanics, and a guy on the bridge.

The destroyer didn't sink, though. They had to bring a huge tow ship to bring both pieces back to the base. So when we went through Gibraltar, everybody was awake and outside, and since the accident was very recent, everyone was scared.

We arrived in Brittany and celebrated for a day or two in the bars. We had a good time and got pretty drunk. Then I got a new assignment on a minesweeper, La Glycine, as its only cook. There were about thirty personnel on board. That ship went out almost every day of the week, good weather or bad, no matter what. The waves could be twenty feet high and the wind's fierce. We were out where the Atlantic Ocean meets the English Channel. The sea was very rough, especially in winter.

Every week we had a group from naval school come aboard, young kids, sixteen to seventeen years old. They'd sail with us for a week to learnM most of them got sick. In fact, one day the ocean was especially bad. I was outside; the kids were out there, too. I went down the stairs to my kitchen. One kid opened the door and was coming up. The force of the waves both pushes you down and pushes you up. The kid was struggling to get up the stairs. The downward force of the sea reversed; he leaped four stairs and threw up all over me, which made me sick, too. We both threw up all over the bulkhead.

My onboard kitchen was small. The stove was maybe four by four. It had bars to contain the pots and pans. The burner was electric and all flat. You could cook for six to eight places. There was an oven. I tried not to keep my pots filled up too much. Sometimes it was difficult to set the table and keep cooking. The officers came into the kitchen and served themselves. It was a small section. There were two tables: one for six or seven officers, the rest for sailors. The commandant was one of two officers who ate alone in quarters built for two.

I took care of the officers in the first month because they knew I was a better cook. On the minesweeper, everyone ate the same meal, including the commandant. I enjoyed that posting because I was able to make my own menu. I served whatever I wanted to, including liver and coq au vin. When it was bitter cold in the winter, they always asked me to make hot wine with fruit inside, like oranges and apples. I added ratafia (unrefined rum) to bring out the alcohol more. It could be as low as 22 to 25 degrees outside. You took a shot from a glass to keep warm and keep working. We always kept two or three liters available. The wine wasn't very good. And with the ship's motion, it kept sloshing around in its steel containers.

I spent a good eight or nine months on that ship. At night we dropped anchor close to the coast, maybe two or three miles. So you could see it. There was no minesweeping unless we needed to go back home. In the morning the commandant expected his croissant, coffee, and a newspaper. Along with a mechanic, I'd put a little boat with an engine on the water early in the morning—six, six thirty—and we'd sail to the village to buy bread, croissants, and a newspaper. I was privileged to go ashore, unlike everybody else. I'd come back and make the coffee for the commandant. As the bakeries were all within half a block of the port, I didn't get to see the entire village. I could only be there for only ten minutes or so before we had to get back to the ship. Later, we'd cut anchor and sail up to forty miles a day performing minesweeping and navigation exercises for young cadets.

I don't regret military life. It taught me discipline, responsibility, and organization. I had a good time. But I didn't want to spend my life as a prisoner. I wanted to be free. I enjoyed friendships with guys who were the same age as me.

My service ended in April of '72, after fourteen months. When a group of us left, I had a duffel bag full of clothes. I drew pictures of a naked woman on it. We left from Brest, five of us getting out at the same time. My house at Avignon was the farthest away, maybe twelve hundred kilometers. The closest one among the five of us was from Brest. We dropped him there and spent time inside the town, staying the night together, drinking at his house. Then four of us said bye-bye and left. Two guys were from Paris, so we spent another day and a night there. Again, the same thing, drinking, blah-blah-blah. Then we left them there. Now we were only two, and the other guy was from Lyon. So we went all the way down to Lyon, and again together we drank and drank. So basically, we were out for four straight days, drinking day and night, sleeping maybe an hour or two. I don't know how I got back home. My liver was big from too much alcohol. But I was young doing stupid things. I couldn't do that anymore.

That was the last of me and the Navy.

Time to Pursue My Culinary Aspirations

$\mathcal{I}$ was happy to be home, but it felt strange. I had been gone for over a year doing military duties. But I had to get back to work. I stayed home for maybe a week or ten days before I went back to work in a different restaurant than the one I worked in earlier. Le Prieure was its name, which refers to a cloister from the sixteen hundreds, transformed into a hotel. It was located in a small village near Avignon, across the Rhone River, called Villeneuve les Avignon. That's where I worked for a little more than one year. The hotel had about forty-five rooms, a pool, and a highly regarded restaurant with one Michelin star.

In Spring 1972, a good friend from the Navy lived in a small village nearby; we had lunch there. It felt good to be back in the area with my family close by and friends I hadn't seen for a year and a half. Most of my pleasure was in going back to doing what I liked to do, which was cooking and still learning. I liked Le Prieure because the chef, Michel, there was very skilled. He taught me different techniques and more about pastry, because their pastry chef was also good. I didn't know how to make croissants or brioche until then. I learned different recipes. It offered a lighter cuisine, a little more avant-garde, like serving whole fish and carving it in front of diners. The basics were the same, of course, but the stove was different too. Most stoves were gas and electric, but this one was coal. We had to make sure to maintain the coal in the stove, which required another technique, and keep the temperature going.

So this was different. Plus it was a hotel restaurant. We had to deal with guests from the hotel, who came in maybe for a week. Every day it was the same people wanting new dishes. We had to learn their habits, so the menu changed every day.

I had an opportunity to go to Paris, work for the Taillevent, a three Michelin star restaurant, but instead I took a job in St. Tropez because I wanted to enjoy life on the Riviera. So I went to the Byblos, which is also a five-star hotel, and there I learned quite a bit. I had more responsibility. I became chef de partie in charge of the sauces and called chef saucier, which is the chef responsible for most of the sauces. It was also a one-star Michelin restaurant and also a Lebanese restaurant. So I learned from a Lebanese chef. It was a completely different style of cuisine. You had to make a shish kebab, and how to make a tabouli, which I'd never even seen before. It was all new to me, like how to prepare eggplants, which I'd also never done before. They required different techniques such as roasting eggplant, learning new spices, and how to combine them for different flavors, and using yogurt for marinating meat and poultry. There were some similarities between French and Lebanese cuisine, both being Mediterranean and involving the use of garlic and olive oil. Grilling was essential to this form of cooking too.

I found a room. I could not afford more than that. It was one of four rented rooms in a house. At the hotel, I met the hostess of the restaurant. She was an American. Her name was Melissa. After a month or so, I started to go out with her and fell in love. I asked her if she wanted to move in with me so at least we could share our rent. So she moved in, and we became very much in love together, from the winter to May or so. This was 1973, and a big turn in my life was getting ready to start a new venture.

She was studying at the university at Aix-en-Provence. She worked weekends and made the hour-and-a-half trip to university, spending three days and then coming back. She wanted to become a French teacher in the States. Her visa was expiring at the end of May, so she needed to go back to the US.

"Are you coming with me?" she asked.

I said, "I don't think so, because the summer season here is very active until mid-September, and I cannot leave the job just like that. It would be bad for everybody, and my career."

So the time arrived for her to leave.

She was a Christian, too, and she wanted to see Lourdes where the Virgin Mary appeared several times to a young poor girl, Bernadette, and many miracles occurred there since then. It was the end of May. She didn't have much money because she was working only two or three days a week and she had to pay for the trip home. So I paid for the trip to Lourdes, three days for the hotel and stuff, and then I bought quite a lot of souvenirs for her parents and brother.

She was from Sun Valley, 20 minutes from downtown L.A. Though she was leaving, I didn't think we were breaking up. I told her to write to me when she got home, look for a job for me, and let me know about her progress. I wouldn't be able to go over until October because I wanted to finish the season in St. Tropez. She said okay. At the time we didn't have Internet and cell phones. My parents did not have the telephone yet at home. We barely got a TV.

She left. Communication was very poor. I was busy working morning, noon, and night, twelve to fifteen hours a day. There was no time to write. I worked six days a week, and when I was off, I was tired and had to do laundry and so many other things.

Around July I got a letter saying she was looking for a job for me, but it was difficult. Then I didn't receive anything. I said to myself, "Well, I need to go ahead and start to get ready to leave." I didn't want to go by myself because I spoke no English whatsoever. I didn't care much about that because I would be with her. I asked another chef de partie named Serge Almeras if he would like to come with me to the United States and maybe work there for a few months together. I had to convince him over time. Finally he agreed.

I didn't have much money, and I still had to pay rent and other expenses. The little bit of savings I had wasn't much, and I had already spent a lot on the trip to Lourdes and all those gifts. I bought a car, a Renault, so I could go back once in a while to see my mom. When it got to the end of September, I stopped going out with friends like I used to do, just to save my money. They all thought I was crazy, wondering what I had to go to the US for. They were against my decision. I told my mom and dad that I was preparing to leave. On the way back from Lourdes, Melissa and I spent a day or two in my mother's house. I told my mom I wanted to go to the States to be with Melissa and then I'd come back with her. I wouldn't be gone long. She was not too happy. It was so far, so dangerous; Melissa would need a visa to return. I don't remember all the specifics, but it was difficult for her. So I just said, "Mom, I'm going to go."

DOVER SOLE "PETRACQUE" FROM LE PRIEURE

4 serving

Ingredients

4 ea. whole dover sole (about 18 oz.)

2 cup of dry vermouth (Noilly Prat)

1 cup of fish fumet (fish bone stock)

6 oz. butter

6 oz. parmesan cheese, grated very fine

Preparation

Clean well under cold water the dover sole, remove the gut, and with a scissor, trim the fin all around. Remove the dark skin, and leave the white skin on the sole. Cut the head off. Place the dover sole in a long enough shallow dish, oven proof, lightly buttered. Pour the vermouth and the fish fumet over the sole. Cover it with aluminum foil, cook it in the oven at 400 degrees, for about 15 to 20 minutes. Once cooked, remove the sole with a spatula, set it on a cutting board, and transfer the cooking liquid in a saucepan over high heat. Let reduce to almost glace. In the meantime, with a spoon and a fork, remove the central bone from the sole by sliding the spoon from head to tail, between the flesh and the bone. Slide the top 2 filet on the cutting board, remove the bone, and then put back the 2 filet on top of the other 2 from the bottom. Place the sole in an oven-proof dish, cover the sole with parmesan cheese, pack it well with your fingertips. Once the reduction is almost as a glaze, whisk the butter into the glaze over low heat. Pour the mixture over the sole, and place the dish under a broiler for up to 3 minutes until it is nice and light brown. Serve it immediately. Bon appetit!

Taking a Chance

October came, and I sold my car. The difference between what I owed and what I got was maybe $500. With that money, I planned to fly to Los Angeles. I had three hundred and fifty dollars left. I thought Melissa would have found a job for me. I didn't tell my mom about that, but my plan was to stay there once I arrived.

I quit my job in October, went back home, and prepared to leave. I bought a round-trip plane ticket for mid-November.

Serge's friend's village was about an hour from Avignon. We bought our tickets together to leave from Paris so my parents and my sister could accompany us to Orly Airport where we boarded the plane, a Boeing 727. This was my first time flying.

Before that, in October, I sent a letter to Melissa to tell her what day we were leaving and when we were scheduled to arrive at LAX. I missed her. I was looking forward to seeing her and spending the rest of my life with her.

We took off. After seven or eight hours of flying, we had to land in the American Midwest somewhere to refuel. Then we flew on to LAX.

It was a very long trip.

When we arrived, I thought she'd be there to greet us. The airport was small in '73. So we picked up our suitcases and walked out, expecting to see her. No Melissa anywhere. I thought maybe she was late. I could not call her since I didn't have her phone number. We waited a half hour, an hour, two hours.

I said to Serge, "We cannot stay here forever. Let's go to a hotel and then see what we will do."

We were tired. It had been a long trip. It was late afternoon already. I didn't know that the taxi here is called a cab. In French, it's taxi. In France I'd seen a movie that was shot in New York. It showed taxis everywhere. "Yellow cabs," they were called. That's what they must be here, I thought.

When the first one arrived, this huge African American guy got out. He must have been 6'3". He took our suitcases, put them in the trunk, closed it, and we got in.

He asked (I guessed), "Where do you want to go?"

"Hotel! Hotel!"

The guy asked (I guessed), "Which one?"

"Hotel!" We didn't know anything, so we couldn't answer. He stopped the cab, got out, opened the trunk, and put our suitcases out on the street. We got out, and he left.

What do we do now? After fifteen minutes or so, a lady came over to us speaking English. In French, I told her I was sorry, I didn't speak any English.

Then she said, "I speak French. I am French Canadian. I work at the Avis rent-a-car here at the airport and I saw you through the window. I saw the taxi put you out, so I came to see if you need help."

I told her that we were waiting for a girl to pick us up and she hadn't come and I didn't have the phone number and I don't know where she is. I don't even know if she got my letter or not. We didn't know where to go.

The woman said, "Stay here. There are a lot of hotels around the airport; we can call one and they'll pick you up and you will see the name of the hotel on the van."

We waited ten or fifteen minutes. The van arrived and took us to the hotel. The guy at the lobby asked us, "What kind of room do you want, with shower, no shower? With a bath?"

I want a room; who cares? We didn't know what he was asking, showing us this and that on the map. The first night we spent some forty dollars. I said, "My God, I have only $350."

Anyway, we spent the night. In the morning, I was hungry, so I said, "Let's have breakfast."

I was expecting, like in France, coffee, croissants, bread, jam, something like that. So we went to the restaurant's coffee shop. Oh my God. We saw cooks with red hats, only African-American guys working there, and people eating potatoes, eggs, and big pieces of sausage, bacon, and steak.

I thought, *What is that? Is it time to eat lunch now?* It was early morning. We didn't know people ate that kind of food in the morning.

We sat down at the counter. We didn't know what to do. I drank some coffee and ate some white bread. I remember the smell of everything, the fried potatoes. Ah, it was disgusting in the morning. The coffee was terrible. In France you have cafe crème, cappuccino. At the time, cappuccino didn't even exist here. The coffee—you could see through it.

We paid and went back to the room. Then we wondered about what we could do. I said, "What if we look at the phone book?" I looked to see if there's a French restaurant listed. I needed to speak to somebody who speaks French. So I looked in the phone book and found the name of a French restaurant, Chantal, in Santa Monica. I went into the phone booth and put in some money, because, again, I assumed it was going to be the same as in France.

"Does somebody there speak French?"

"Ya, ya, I do."

I explained what happened to me, the girlfriend, et cetera. He said, "Oh, you have an accent from the south of France. Where are you from?"

"Avignon. "

"There's a wine salesman here right now from Avignon. Wait I'll call him."

So, the guy comes to the phone, asks me my name, what am I doing here. I told him I am a chef, I came from Avignon, I worked at the Hiely Lucullus. Right away we made a connection. He asked me if I knew his brother who also worked at Hiely Lucullus, and of course I did. He knew my mother also. I told him where I was and didn't know where to go. He said, "I will pick you up in the next couple of hours. Wait there."

He arrived two or three hours later in an antique French Citroen Traction from the Second World War, circa 1944-45. He'd brought it over on a ship from France and drove it from New York to L.A. He'd been in the country since the mid'60s, so he had already been here for eight or nine years. He'd been a waiter and in the past two years a wine salesman. So he knew a lot of restaurants in the area.

He took us to his house and said, "Don't worry. I know a lot of restaurants around here. It should be easy to find a job. Chefs like you are rare, and there are people who will love to have you."

He left, came back that night, and said, "I have some options. Tomorrow we'll go for an interview."

And we went. Boom, first interview. "Okay, you're in."

The name of the restaurant was St. Tropez. It was located on Santa Monica Boulevard near Century City.

I was surprised the first day on the job to see what kind of food they were serving. I was expecting the kind of nice food we have in France. With the name St. Tropez, I thought maybe they served Mediterranean or Provence cuisine. Oh my God, it was terrible to the point that, when I saw salmon on the menu, I had to ask how it's prepared. I don't remember the specifics, but the salmon came from a can, spooned directly onto the plate. I'd never seen salmon in a can before. I've seen tuna in France, but I'd never seen salmon. This was another surprise.

Everything, including the vegetables, was frozen in a bag. The only thing they made fresh was cheesecake. And cheesecake I'd never seen before in my life either. The owner would come in late in the afternoon with a cheesecake, which he'd made at home.

So that was my first day, my first experience. I stayed there for two or three weeks, but I was not happy. I wanted to teach the owner some dishes I had been making in France. Would he let me do it? No, no, no, we had to do it this way.

The economy was very bad at this time. The country was going through a recession in November and December of '73, so they couldn't pay me much. I made only $20.00 a day. After three weeks, the old man came to me and said, "I have to let you go, because we have no customers. We have maybe fifteen or twenty covers a night, and I cannot pay you anymore."

So I left. My salesman friend said, "Don't worry. There are plenty of other restaurants." A couple of days later he found me something else, a restaurant called Deux Crepes. The lady who owned it thought she could serve a menu of about fifteen different crepes, savory and sweet.

The cooler was terrible. Everything was on the floor. There were no shelves. It was a little store. And my gosh, she was buying chicken that had already been cooked and frozen and put in a small bag. It was terrible. I wondered why I was there, looking for a way out from the moment I started work.

I stayed there for a week or two. She couldn't make it either and closed the door. I found a better job in an Italian restaurant in Century City called Harry's Bar. That was a true restaurant. The food was better, the chef was from England, everything was more delicate, including the sauces. It was busy. I felt more in my element.

Time went by. I'd been in the States for nine weeks and already had three jobs. I was concerned about my girlfriend. She didn't know I was here. I'd told my friend that we needed to find an apartment. By now we had saved a little money from working. But I needed to find her. I missed her so much.

I had her address. It was in Sun Valley. My friend said it was far but we'd go together and chose the next day.

We set out, and when we got to her place, he knocked on the door and a woman opened it. I think it was her mother. He explained to her who I was and that I was looking for Melissa. There were steps in front of the door. She called inside, saying, "You have someone here to see you." Melissa came down the stairs but at first couldn't see me standing outside. When she did, her eyes grew wide. She was surprised to see me and stood for a few seconds before she came down and said, "Oh my God, what are you doing here?"

I thought she was joking. "What do you mean, what am I doing here?" All this was spoken in French.

"You knew very well I was coming. I sent you the letter with the details of the trip, my flight number, and time of arrival, etcetera, we have been together for almost a year, I was so happy, so in love, all that stuff."

"I didn't know you were so serious. If only I knew, blah blah blah . . . I have my boyfriend here. We're going to get married."

What?

I felt like somebody had stabbed me. I couldn't believe what she was saying. I couldn't think of a reply. I was shocked. I started to cry. I couldn't speak. I told my friend, "Let's go." And we left.

He laughed in the car on the way back. I told him, "You don't understand. I left my family. My mother cried and worried. I went to the other side of the world where I didn't know the language. I had no job. I came just for her, and look what happened!"

I couldn't believe it.

I had two choices: stay or go back to France. But because of my ego, I choose to stay, to avoid humiliation from all my friends back home.

Santa Monica, Le Saint Michel

ore time passed. I went on working. I was angry at women. For a few weeks I went with my friend Serge to discotheques and felt, "Nah." I joked with girls but didn't respect them. A couple of months went by before I began to feel better.

In the meantime, we were invited to a Mardi Gras celebration in the French community. We went to meet more French countrymen, and there I met a guy who wanted to open a restaurant. He said he'd heard about me and asked if I'd be willing to work for him. I said, "Sure, why not?" He told me I could come to work for him in two weeks or a month, so I said, "Okay, great."

We made an agreement, and I went to work for him in a restaurant called Le Saint Michel located at Santa Monica Boulevard and Bundy drive. Its specialty was duck and fish only. I said, "That's fine; we will create an exciting menu."

When I came to the restaurant for the first time, and I saw the kitchen, I was very surprised to see how small it was. It was about 12 x 10 feet, with two very old stoves, a steam table, and a pantry refrigerator. I told myself, "It has to work. I will make it work." After a couple of days of preparation, we opened the restaurant. We did well the first couple of weeks, but after that we tapered off, doing anywhere from five to fifteen guests. Then we got a nice article from Lois Dwan, the food critic for the *Los Angeles Times*. She was well known in Hollywood.

Boom! The week after the article came out, we were packed. The phone rang and rang and rang. We went from doing twenty covers a night to doing a hundred and forty, a hundred and fifty, in a restaurant that seated forty-eight, with no bar. It was something I'd never seen before in my life. People waited in the street for an hour for a table. We didn't have a waiting room.

The customers were happy and kept coming back. The business flourished. It didn't take too long before I got some press interested in my cuisine, my style. So I got nice articles in the *Hollywood Reporter, Los Angeles Magazine*, and *Newsweek*. I felt great to be recognised for what I loved to do: cooking and pleasing my guests.

You opened the door, there was the podium, and you were in the restaurant. People waiting in the street, I swear, for an hour was something I'd never seen in my life. In France, no one waits in the street to get into a restaurant. Forget it. You come back the next day. But here in the States, that was another thing that shocked me. I thought only crazy people would wait for an hour and a half to get a table in a restaurant. It was difficult, but we had great success with that restaurant for quite a few years. I don't know how I could pull it off, doing so many covers with two helpers and minimal equipment in a kitchen of 120 square feet.

A lot of showbiz customers from Hollywood came in. We had Steve McQueen who, at the time, was pretty ill with cancer. I bought a six-pack of special beer for him at the liquor store across the street every time he came for dinner. Ali McGraw and Candace Bergen always asked for their special salad dressing on the side. Robert Redford and Dustin Hoffman who dined at the restaurant the night before he won an Oscar for *Kramer vs. Kramer*. Ronald Reagan before presidency, the entire crew of "Young Frankenstein"—Mel Brooks, Gene Wilder, Marty Feldman and their group, which consisted of Anne Bancroft, Don de Luis and Burt Reynolds—they all came in three times a week, for months. I even spent time with them after dinner. Gene continued to visit the restaurant after filming wrapped. He used to go to the restaurant I worked at in France. He got to know me and came into the kitchen to say hello every now and then and gave me a bottle of Bordeaux wine to celebrate when my son was born. George Lucas was a regular before he did "Star Wars." The famous architect Frank Gehry was a regular; every Wednesday for three or four years, he ate the same dish, red snapper grenobloise.

Every day I prepared more than 40 whole ducks, fresh from a farm outside LA. Making five different sauces for it depended on the season, while using different fruits: apricots, peaches, cherries, apples and pears, plus wild mushroom chanterelles, trumpets and porcini with aged madeira. The fish was fresh every day, some of it local, such as swordfish, red snapper and bass; some was from Mexico (huachinango, corvina) or Alaska (Halibut, king crabs and black cod).

I had carte blanche to buy anything I wish to put on the menu. It was sometimes difficult to find the right product as a minimum was imported from France at that time, but I managed to make it work. It was a dream job. I enjoyed creating my own dishes. I even made my own pastries for dessert, simple desserts, like apple tart tatin, berry tart, chocolate mousse cake, tira-misu, cream puff, coffee, vacherin and floating island. I wish I could have a sorbet machine to make my own ice cream. I saw in the dishwasher a great interest to learn how to cook, so I took the time to train him to be a kitchen helper. I can see that he was passionate and he became very good at it, so good that ten years later he was hired as the chef for a small French restaurant in Studio City.

During that first year, I was illegal in the country, working without a permit. It was risky. One day, just before I got to work, the immigration agents came to the restaurant for control. Two came from the front door and two from the back door. It was during the lunch hour, the only cook at that time was my sous chef. He was taking care of the lunch. He was a French Canadian illegal as well. After questioning him, the agents took him away, and my boss had to take over in the kitchen. Lucky me, I came about fifteen minutes later to start to work for the dinner service. Few days later, I heard that my sous chef was deported back to Canada. I never saw him again. I was worried that immigration would come back, so I really did everything I could to have my papers in order with the help of a couple of lawyers. Yes, it cost me a bunch at that time, but it was worth it. Finally, in May 1975, I got my Green Card, another God blessing.

Maria, nickname Cuca

*L*ife got sweeter when in the spring of 1974 I met the girl who would become my wife. Serge and I moved into a two-bedroom apartment situated on Clark Street, just above the Whisky a Go Go in West Hollywood. I bought a car from my boss, a used Volvo. Serge had an MG that was always breaking down. He was going to school twice a week to learn English. He tried to push me to go to school with him, but I was not interested. I was not a school guy.

One day he came home and said, "Sunday we're going to San Diego Sea World with a girl I met in school. Can you come with us? I'll tell her to bring a girl for you."

The reason he wanted me to go with them was that my car was better than his. So we picked up the girl at her sister's house in Burbank. Her name was Maria del Refugio Sandoval, but she went by the nickname Cuca.

On the way there, Serge rode in the back and Cuca rode in the front. Communication was poor. I barely spoke a few words in English. I only knew a few words. But on the way back, I could feel something happen between Cuca and me. She would look at me and smile, telling me stuff I didn't understand. Then my friend said, "Let's go home." He spoke better English because he'd been to school for two months. He said, "Let's celebrate the evening with a glass of wine in the apartment. We have some cheese." He invited Cuca, so the three of us shared a glass of wine and some cheese.

We talked, myself adding a couple of words here and there. I could feel the attraction between both of us.

We went to drop Cuca to her sister's house, and the next day I told Serge that maybe it'd be a good idea for me to go to school because I could learn to speak better English. So he introduced me to his teacher. We went to class in the morning, and Cuca was there.

We started to see each other and communicate better. I became attracted to her more and more. I felt so grateful. Two weeks went by like that, including a few days of classes. I told Serge that she was in love with me. He was a little upset. He wanted to be with her, but he was not her style. So Cuca and I began to see each other. I went to her house; she came to mine. My English was getting better. I knew she was Mexican. She was here for one year to learn English to get a better job as executive secretary for the firm Datsun and planned to go back to Mexico. But we were getting serious about each other. We fell in love and moved into an apartment together.

She spent some time explaining some Mexican food, like corn tortillas, guacamole, enchiladas and a few more dishes, but I never had a taste of it. One day, I went to pick her up at her friend's house. She was cooking some gorditas (small cups made of fresh masa, filled with beans and topped with some cheese, baked in the oven for a few minutes). She invited me to have one. I could not refuse. I bit on it. Just the smell of the corn tortillas and the cilantro almost threw me up. I was embarrassed, so I turned my back to her and put the rest in the pocket of my jacket. Cuca then asked me if I liked it. Of course I said yes. My taste buds were not ready for those new ingredients, such as corn tortillas or cilantro. I could not stand the smell or the taste of it. It took me a while to get used to those new products.

Within a year, Cuca and I started to talk about meeting each other's family. We got engaged in a quick dinner ceremony in a French restaurant. I made her eat escargot and frog legs. She didn't know what she was eating, but she enjoyed it very much and then decided to get married. She announced it to her family, and we drove to Mexico in my Volvo. It was a white, kind of beige, color. I went to Earl Scheib to give it a quick coat of navy blue, almost black, and I said, "This will be our car for the wedding, instead of a limo."

It was a long drive going through the desert of Sonora until we stopped at Mazatlan, then Puerto Vallarta. I got sick from drinking ice tea (the water there was contaminated). After five days, we crossed Mexico City, before going to Cuernavaca (50 miles south of Mexico City), where I met the entire family. Of course they spoke only Spanish, which I couldn't understand. But Cuca translated for me, so after I met her mom and dad and her eight siblings. It was time to organize the wedding. We arranged for the photographer and the ceremony. I spent some time with my future father-in-law, trying to speak Spanish to him and understand what he was telling me. We went to discover some antique small villages and different Mercado (street markets where they sell all kinds of products and made-to-order street food). I first tried a pulque, a fermented drink made from the sap of the maguey agave, cured with celery and flavored with strawberry or other fruit. It's sweet and can get to your head very quickly. Pulqueria is the name of the place where the pulque is processed; it smelled so bad that I almost puked. Then we went on to try different tequilas and mezcal. Then it was time to try a variety of local foods, such as grilled nopales, tacos de jumiles, Caldo de corderos and tacos, all made on the spot with fresh corn tortillas. I was not ready for this. My stomach got upset. But later on I got used to those new tastes and flavors. Now I really enjoyed all those different authentic dishes.

I went on to a golf club, Club Tabachine, in Cuernavaca—very elegant—to book our wedding. Luckily, I was making good money at the time, so I could pay for everything. In Mexico the tradition for a wedding is to get a friend or relative to sponsor an item, i.e., rings, cake, music, the photographer and the bar. The only thing I was responsible for was the food. I met the chef there, and together we created a festive tapas-style reception with some Mexican dishes.

The day of the wedding, July 19, 1975, came. We drove to the cathedral in my navy-blue Volvo and got married. About 200 people came. It was very festive and emotional. Then everyone drove through the streets of the village to the golf club for the reception. Everyone had a great time that lasted until late night. We spent our first night in a small village, Taxco, about 60 miles south of Cuernavaca, which was built over a silver mine. On the way there I had to avoid cows sleeping in the middle of the road. Then I got a flat tire in the middle of nowhere and had to change it at three a.m. in my tuxedo. Our honeymoon lasted for a few days, but it was very memorable and unique for me.

On the way back to Cuernavaca, I suggested that we go to France to get married again because my family couldn't make it here; it was too expensive to fly everybody over. I hadn't told my mom and dad that I was already married. I just said that I was bringing my girlfriend and we were planning to get married. My mom wondered how Cuca's parents could let her go like that beforehand. My parents are very Catholic. My mother would never accept me getting married without the family being there.

When we arrived in France, I presented Cuca to my parents as my girl-friend. She didn't speak any French and my family didn't speak any Spanish or English, so it was a huge challenge of communication. My mom was very patient with Cuca. She took her time to teach her some French, but after a week or so, Cuca went to a school to learn French and things were getting better. As good Catholics, we had to sleep in separate bedrooms. At night, when everyone was asleep, I'd go see her. We did that for a few months. Cuca understood because she was Catholic, too.

Here we were again, organizing for the second wedding. But this time I let my mom take care of most of it. She was very proud and happy to have her son back and getting married, so she took her time doing all the preparation for the wedding and really enjoyed doing so. The wedding was October 4th,

1975. It was a nice ceremony in the church where I was once an altar boy, followed by a beautiful traditional dinner in an old farm near Avignon. All my relatives and friends were there.

Before we went to France, I communicated with my former boss from the Hiely Lucullus. He told me his sister had married someone who was wealthy and wanted to open a small hotel with a nice restaurant.

"Are you willing to come back and handle the opening for them?" he asked.

"Yeah, that's great because I'm going back to get married, so maybe we can do the opening at the same time."

And that's what we did. When we went back to France, right away I went to see about the job before we were even married again. I started to work on the opening for them. It was a very beautiful rustic restaurant, with about thirty seats inside, another fifteen or twenty outside and about twenty-five rooms in the hotel which was called La Genestiere. It had tennis courts, a pool and a huge park and was located at Monteux in the foothills of Mont Ventoux, 25 miles from Avignon.

I formed a team in the kitchen. I had an assistant and two younger cooks. We had a successful opening. People liked it. The cuisine was typically Provençale, with some products from Corsica, but most of it was local, which I always like to take directly from the farms.

Three times a week I went back to the big market at Avignon and met the actual farmers, which was an experience for me. My wife helped me in the hotel where we were given lodging. She did some bookkeeping, a bit of everything. We had a great time. I enjoyed coming back to my roots, putting local flavor into the food. I couldn't do that in the States.

The culinary roots I refer to go back to the flavors of Provence, using game during the winter season—rabbits, partridge, squab or veal kidney and sweet bread—which I couldn't do in the States. It was like giving toys to a kid who's never had them. I felt ow, even though it was hard. We worked two shifts, fourteen hours a day.

My first boss, Pierre Hiely, came to see his sister. I arranged to make a special dish for him from the past. He loved a kidney with whiskey and a special sauce. He came into the kitchen to say hi, and surprisingly, he told me that it was the best kidney he'd ever had. I felt great to hear that from my former boss who once threw a plate in my face. That statement gave me more confidence and courage to keep going. He realized I'd stepped up a lot.

I was happy at that hotel. I had a little car. I enjoyed the scenery with my wife and visiting different places. We had a great time for about ten months. The restaurant was doing well.

But then we decided to move back to the States because I needed to make a better living. The US had a better lifestyle in terms of working conditions than in France. In California, you worked eight or nine hours a day instead of fourteen or fifteen. In France, it took three months' salary just to be able to buy a TV. I could see right away that it was a different lifestyle. It was a lot easier in the US. That's why we decided to come back. Also, I couldn't wait any longer because of my Green Card which is good for only one year if you leave the country.

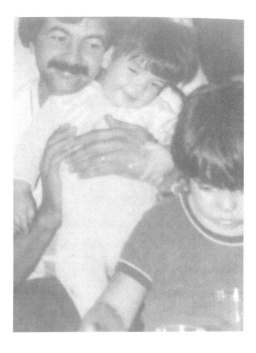

Restaurant Le Canard

We came back and I returned to my job at St. Michel. The place had become a disaster. My style of cooking had always leaned toward the basics. The boss knew the chef who was hired to replace me. But the guy took the job basically for the money. He didn't do much, and he drank a case of beer a day. By eight o'clock at night, he was already drunk. The food was either tasteless, or salty, or overcooked. It was always bad. There were a lot of complaints.

In those ten months, the restaurant lost customers, 50 percent of the old business in all. The owner, Paul Guillemin, was very happy that I came back and advertised it among the clientele. It took a while to regain some of the business because other restaurants had opened in the meantime. We regained our footing, but it was never the same as before we left.

As soon as my wife and I returned, we took an apartment in West Hollywood. She had gotten pregnant. The business was coming back.

I met a steady customer one day in the dining room. He was a wealthy guy. He'd made his money in the hair product industry and had a few hair salons in Canada.

He came to me one day and said, "We should open a business together. Here is the concept: a hair salon for ladies, attached to a fancy restaurant. You will take care of the food; I'll take care of the salon. After their hair is done, you can fix a beautiful breakfast or lunch or a nice complete tea service."

This was going to be in Santa Monica, at the site of an old pizzeria that had a lot of parking space. He was going to put in all the money.

But I was scared because of my wife's pregnancy, which was already four months along. I worried about that and what I'd do if the business didn't work out. I thought about it for a few weeks and finally went to the guy and said, "I'm sorry I've got to turn down your offer. I'm scared."

The restaurant never happened. It was me or nobody.

I had quite a few opportunities like this one. Another guy, who owned the building next to the restaurant, wanted to open a take-out place. We'd only do fresh stuff; it'd be a big menu. But again, oh my gosh, I was scared. So it didn't happen. Then my son Georges was born, April 6, 1977. My parents came from France, for the first time taking a plane and their first time in America. It was a bit overwhelming for them, the size of the city, the traffic, especially coming from a very small town. But I had friends who could take them out, because I was so busy at work. They had a good time in their four or five weeks with us. They helped Cuca with cleaning and preparing food.

I kept working at St Michel for a few more years. Being a father was another responsibility. I loved my son, but I was way too absorbed in my work. I didn't spend the time I really should have with him. When I got up in the morning, instead of helping Cuca, I thought of what I had to do for that day at the restaurant, creating, designing specials, always looking for new products, etc. I'd go to work late mornings and wouldn't come back until eleven at night.

One day a lady came into the restaurant by the name of Madame Claude. She didn't introduce herself, but she was the most famous madam in Europe, with a high-priced clientele that included the Kennedys and Rockefellers, movie stars and celebrities. Her girls were elegant, beautiful, well trained, discreet and expensive. I think the lowest rate was fifteen hundred dollars a night or so, she once told me. Everyone knew Madame Claude, or who she said she was, had to flee Paris because she owed a few millions dollars of back taxes to the French government.

She became a regular customer, coming in two or three times a week. One night she asked to meet the owner, Paul. He was part owner. He came out to meet her. He was originally from Algeria. She told him that she wanted to invest in a small place, similar to St. Michel. She really liked that place, including the food and atmosphere. It was a typical French bistro.

She saw that this place was successful and thought, because of that, he might be able to help her open up another one like it as a partner. She would deposit money in a bank, and when he found a place, he could open it.

This was in '78. She put forty thousand dollars, cash, into a bank as an initial investment.

But Paul was very eccentric. He liked to show off in high society. As much as he made money in a day, he'd spend all of it and more, every day.

So he spent the entire $40,000 deposit of $40,000 and didn't look for the new place.

Time went by, and Mme. Claude came back, a month or two later. She asked about the new place. He told her that it wasn't easy to find. He needed more money; forty thousand isn't enough. So she gave him thirty or forty thousand more through the bank and told him, "I'll give you a certain amount of time, three weeks. But I need to see a place."

She put conditions on the agreement, so Paul rushed to find a site. He took the first cheap location he found and did it without thinking or forming a business plan. He was in a rush from M. Claude's pressure, so he put a new carpet on the floor before he painted the walls. He did everything upside down without thinking.

The place was in Sherman Oaks and would be called Le Canard. He still had to put in tables and find Chinaware.

He ran out of money again, but this time he couldn't ask her for more. He needed a chef. That's when he came to see me. He said, "Look, I have something to ask you. I think it's a great, great opportunity for you. Would you be willing to open a restaurant with me?"

I said, "Yeah. Okay." I felt more confident now, and I didn't want to refuse the offer.

He explained to me the conditions. We would have twenty four and a half percent each of the business, him and I, and the lady would have the rest fifty one percent.

I said okay, but first I want to see the place. He took me to the restaurant. He opened the front door, and I could already see that there was shit everywhere, a brand-new carpet with boxes all over, pieces of drywall on the floor, paint, wires, all kinds of stuff. He took me in the back to see the kitchen. That, for me, was more important. When I saw it, I got stung!

The kitchen consisted of one sink, a hood, a large reach-in and four walls.

"And you want to open when?" I said. "There's not even a stove. What are you going to open with? There's nothing here."

St. Michel was successful because it served good food and had good service, and Paul's partner was smart. But Paul was the kind of guy who could take two thousand dollars out of the cash register at night and spend it all by morning. All the invoices were paid by the partner. They had a lot of fights. I could hear them go at it from the kitchen. Paul was partying, inviting a lot of people to expensive restaurants, ordering a lot of expensive champagne. He drove a nice car. He bought a house in Pacific Palisades. He could blow through $8,000 a week. He was a crazy guy. He never had money in his pocket. He put nothing in the bank. Everything went out the window.

He didn't organize his money, so when it came to the new restaurant, he thought he could do the same thing as he did with St. Michel. Then he told me that, since I had become a partner, I should buy a used stove and grill with my own cash. I had only five thousand dollars in my savings. That was all. We went shopping for used equipment and put all my money into buying what we could. We planned to create the same menu as at St. Michel, mainly duck and seafood. Four weeks went by when Mme. Claude asked to see the place. We were ready to open the following week.

We opened in early '78, without publicity, without any advance notice. The first week we served around 10 diners a night. Of those diners, four were people Paul invited. We may have made $200 a night, but we had one hundred-and-fifty dollars in food costs alone, plus everything else.

We went on like this for maybe three weeks. In the meantime, I had no money. I asked Paul for a pay check. He said, "You're the boss now, so if there's no money, you have to wait." So I waited a few more days, but I had to pay the rent, food and gas. I asked one friend to lend me five hundred dollars, another two hundred. Everyone was helping me as best they could.

I waited a couple more weeks. I said to Paul, "Look, I need to get paid."

He said, "When we're only serving eight people, what can I do? It takes time," blah blah blah. Six or seven weeks went by. I had a friend who was a lawyer, not a part of the corporation we'd formed. I explained what was going on to him.

He said, "Get out of there. You will never make a penny back. Get out before it's too late." Knowing Paul the way he was, I shouldn't have ever accepted to be his partner.

I went to see Paul the next morning. I said, "Look, if you don't give me a pay check today, I won't come back to work. I've been here for seven or eight weeks without getting paid. I have to survive. I have a wife and a kid."

He got very upset.

My wife told me that I should talk to the lady, Mme. Claude. We should kick Paul out of the way and work together to maintain the place.

But I didn't have the guts to do that. I said, "Forget it." I was really upset. I quit, then I called all my friends to tell them that I had no work. I needed a job.

The next day a friend came back and said, "Guess what? Le Dome restaurant in West Hollywood, right on Sunset blvd, is going to open in a couple of weeks, and they need a chef as the one they had, needed to go back to France."

So I went to meet the owners, as I knew them from before. They hired me right away. Everything was already done for the opening, menus, cooks, suppliers' list; I only had to do some training with the team. We were a good team there, with ten to twelve cooks. We got busy right from the opening. We served 350 to 400 people a night. You'd look at the parking lot and see Rolls-Royces, Maseratis, Porsches, Ferraris.

A lot of people wanted to work there. The owners knew half the restaurants in the city. One of the owners, Michel, was part owner of Le Restaurant on Melrose Place. The other owner, Edith, was part owner of Le St. Germain, the number one local restaurant at the time. They knew the best clientele in Los Angeles, all the jet-set and showbiz people. So when they opened Le Dome, it became a gold mine.

Elton John was a good friend of Michel, who was gay. Once they brought me a bag of marijuana to make cookies in celebration of Elton John's birthday. That was back in '76 when I went to help for the birthday party at Le Restaurant.

Ringo Starr came in often. We had a lot of French singers. It was very busy. This reminded me of the beginning of St Michel; the only difference was I had a closer relationship with celebrities. We enjoyed good reviews.

After a month or two, I'd seen the results of our success. My former boss, Paul, came in for lunch. My boss at Le Dome said, "Paul's come to see you."

I said, "Oh my God. What's he doing here? I don't want to see him." On the third time he came for lunch, he insisted on seeing me, so I went outside to meet. He said it was nice to see me; he'd been missing me. Then he said he needed me back at St. Michel. He proposed paying me X amount of dollars to return. I said, "Wow." I needed this in writing, with a signed statement.

He said he'd met with the CEO of Campbell's soup and wanted me to develop all sorts of sauces for ducks that they would can and sell in supermarkets across the US. It sounded like a good idea, but I told him I wanted to talk to my wife before making a decision. I didn't want to get screwed again.

I turned him down.

He came back another time and said, "Forget about the Campbell soup. If you don't want to do that, I understand, but if you come back to the restaurant, I'll give you more money."

His offer was for a lot more than I was making now. It was a small place, with less headaches. So I said, "Okay, but I want everything in writing." He drew up a letter. Mme. Claude was gone by then. I quit Le Dome after three or four months of working there and went back to St. Michel.

This was in mid to late '78. A year later, we were doing well on the weekends, but it was a struggle on weekdays; it slowed down quite a bit. That's when I started thinking about going back to France to start a new restaurant. It was my dream to have my own business.

I started putting more and more thought into it. I wanted my own place, nobody else's. The only way I could do that financially would be to go back to France, because in France, being a professional, the bank would loan me enough to cover fifty per cent of the business. In the US, the banks are tougher; they don't loan you anything, if you don't already run a business. That was the only way.

We had a Sherman Oaks house by now, which we bought toward the end of 78 and which I fixed up. A customer from Le St Michel, Doctor Lee, who became a good friend, said it was better to buy than to rent. But the house cost about sixty-five thousand dollars, and I didn't have enough for a down payment. I'd only saved five thousand dollars and the down payment was seventy-five hundred. Doctor Lee loaned me the rest and said, 'You can pay me back any way you can.' That was amazing. The house was on Vesper Avenue in Van Nuys. It was beautiful, the only one painted blue in the neighborhood. I worked on it four to five four hours every morning, to make it nicer.

I had the idea to open a Mexican/French restaurant in France, but where? I was thinking of a location that reminds me of tropical weather, palm trees and the ocean, so I thought, *In Nice, on the French Riviera*. It may have been the first Mexican restaurant in France at that time.

Anyway, that was in my dream. But I was still working at St Michel until Paul bought another house and started borrowing more money from the bank. One day I got a pay check, like normal—I got paid every two weeks. I put it in the bank, paid my monthly bills by check and, in a week, everything came back unpaid. The check I received from Paul didn't have funds. When you get unpaid checks from the bank, you have to pay a fee on every one of them.

I was furious. I went back to him and said, "What's going on?"

He said, "I don't understand. I have two accounts. The bank must have drawn from the wrong one."

I said, "I don't care what happened with your bank. You give me the money right now."

So he took a different checking book from another bank and wrote me a check from that account. I took the check to that bank, stood in line for the cashier and gave her the check.

She checked. "Sorry, no funds."

I became furious

I had the key to the restaurant. I was the first to arrive at one p.m. and waited for the crew to arrive at the parking lot in back of the restaurant. They consisted of a couple of cooks, a dishwasher and two servers. I told them I was not opening the door and why: I hadn't been paid in three weeks. "I'm not going to work. Nobody's going to work." They listened and agreed.

Paul arrived about four-thirty p.m. We normally opened the restaurant at five.

"Why haven't you opened?" he asked. "What's going on? You don't have the keys?"

I said, "Listen, Paul. You gave me one check and it bounced. You gave me another one, told me it was good and it bounced again. I'm not going to work. Nobody's going to work, okay? Do you understand?"

"You can't do that! Okay, I'll give you the money. I'm sorry."

"Give me the cash right here, or I'm going to walk."

He was upset. He took the phone and called his wife, a Spanish girl who cooked at home. He said, "Move your ass over here. The stupid chef doesn't want to work. We have to open the restaurant."

As soon as he ended the call, I said, "Paul, I'm the chef here. Nobody gets in and works in my kitchen."

"I understand that. But I'm the boss."

"I don't care if you're the boss. I'm the chef and I'm telling you. You don't come into the kitchen until you pay."

It was severe. The woman arrived and thought she could go into the kitchen. I told her, "Nobody is getting into my kitchen."

He closed the restaurant for the night. The next morning, he came in to apologize and say he had cash for me. I said, "Okay, but I'm not going to work a single day without pay. I want my pay check every night." And that's what he did, straight out of the cash register. We did that every night for three or four months.

That is when I decided to follow my dream and go back to France and open my own restaurant.

My wife was not happy to go. She said, "You have a job here, a car, a house with furniture, two kids—everything you can ask for. Why do you want to go back to France?"

I said, "The government can lend me money to open a restaurant. We can find a place in the French Riviera that's more tropical. We can open a Mexican restaurant that will be the first of its kind in France." She was still not happy about my decision, and after several arguments, she gave up and said fine.

I took a quick trip to France to seek a place in Nice. I didn't really have a chance to study the business, the market or make up a business plan. I did not seek help or guidance; I just followed my instinct.

A friend told me about a person I should meet in Nice. I met him there, and he showed me a couple of places that had possibilities for the restaurant site. I had only a few days to look. But right away I found a place called Chez Grasso and thought it'd be great even though it was kind of far from the ocean, maybe three or four miles east. The rent was not too much, though the place was a mess. It hadn't been used in six years. It was an old restaurant in one of the canyons, in the backcountry. The owner of the property was in his late sixties and wanted to retire with his wife.

It had been a typical French country restaurant, with one set menu and a long family-style table, if you will, and live entertainment. The menu consisted of different crudités and anchoiade (a dressing made of anchovies) and a leg of lamb roasted in the wood oven, served with flageolet, a type of French green kidney beans. There was sauteed herbs and garlic potatoes and a ratatouille from Nice, then a dessert. That was the menu, typical of Nice.

I wanted to have a Mexican restaurant where you enter to find a bar on one side and a few tables, then a main room that seats between seventy and eighty, a corner brick oven perfect for Mexican cuisine and a little terrace with three or four tables. The restaurant would be called Pancho Villa.

There were no other Mexican restaurants in France; in Los Angeles you're already exposed to Mexican food.

On my way back to LA, I was very excited and thought of many things, mainly the decor. The idea then became to go to Mexico and purchase all kinds of objects, including paintings, costumes, sombreros and artisanal potteries. I thought about the design of the main dining room. I would create three or four rows of booths made of stucco to create a small private niche with a look like old Mexican villages. The rest would be family-style tables and then a stage because the prior owner had entertainment. I thought we could do Mariachi there, for ambiance.

Adventures in a 1966 Lincoln Continental

*O*n late spring of 1980, I told my boss I'd leave at the end of June. I gave him two or three weeks' notice, and that was it. I informed my wife of the plan: we would drive into Mexico after selling the house, the furniture, both cars and everything we could. My mom had passed away in 1978, two years prior. She left me a little bit of money. But with this amount and the money from the house, furniture and everything else, we would have enough to buy decor in Mexico, pay for the trip and put about 40% down to open the restaurant, too.

We put the Van Nuys house up for sale in May. Within ten days, it sold for a hundred and fifteen thousand. It was well decorated and well maintained; I'd put a lot of time and effort into it. It looked good. The first person who came to look at it bought it. We got a good profit. We'd bought it for sixty-five thousand and had had it for only two years.

My brother-in-law, Xavier Nunez, offered to sell me his 1966 Lincoln Continental, a huge car, a classic with the suicide doors. You could put four people in the trunk. It would be perfect to take everything with us, as my wife wanted to give all our kitchen utensils to her mother (including the coffee machine, blenders, juicer, toaster, a stereo and speakers, small kitchenware and more).

We put everything in the trunk. We were expecting to leave for good. With the house sold, I put the money in the bank here and wired it to France. I kept a good amount of cash on hand for Mexico. Brian, our second child, was not yet a year old. Georges was about three. We packed the car. The trunk was full and the rest of our belongings piled on the roof in a rack.

Away we went. Our decision was to make the trip in two weeks, as I was planning to get to France at the end of June, early July, in order to take advantage of the summer high season, which would be best for the restaurant.

The itinerary was as follows: to drive along the border all the way to Texas and cross through El Paso-Juarez and continue down all the way to Cuernavaca Morelos (about 2600 miles).

On the way, in the middle of Arizona, I blew a tire. As the spare was in the bottom of the trunk, it became a mess to unload the car in order to change the tire.

I changed it, but the spare was in bad shape. We needed to stop somewhere to get a new tire. After I changed to the spare, we got off the freeway and found a tire shop. The guy said, "Let me put the car on the lift." It could hardly move. He said, "What did you put in your car? It's so heavy." After he changed the tire, he looked up at the others and said, "They're ready to blow up. We need to change all of them."

So we did. I didn't expect the amount of time it would take and the expense in my planning and budget.

But with four new tires, we took off again. We crossed the border in Texas. No one asked us anything. Then, twenty miles further south, there was a second custom revision where the officers checked everything we had in the car. They looked at all this stuff and said, "Where are you going?" I replied that we were going to our house in Mexico City.

He said, "Come with me." I went into the custom office. As they were questioning me, my wife waited in the car with both children, wondering what was going on. I told her that the guy didn't want us to go on with all this stuff; he wanted to take everything out.

I had to give money to the official, fifty dollars, for him to let us go. So there was more money lost and a couple of more hours wasted.

We drove on through the desert.

Just before we approached a small city, late in the afternoon, the back of the car started to make a strange wobbling motion. I stopped to inspect the rear end and saw that one of the wheels had only one bolt left. It looked like they had been cut right at the edge of the wheel, so there was nowhere to screw new ones back on.

We could not go on like this. We were on the side of the road, and traffic was getting bad as people were coming home from work. I tried to wave at a car to stop. Finally one did. My wife explained to the driver what was going on. This was in 1981, before cell phones. The guy said, "I'll go into the city to look for a tow truck to pick you up."

We'd been on the side of the road for maybe two hours, waiting in the car for a tow truck to come. Then we saw an old tow truck approach. It was so old that it had just a chain hanging off of the winch. The guy said, "I'll take you into town." He hooked up the car with the chain, and the four of us got into the truck.

We had to find a Lincoln dealership that knew how to fix a Continental. The closest we could find was a Ford dealership. It was already late, around six o'clock, so the dealership was closed. *What should we do?* I told my wife that we would need to spend the night in a hotel and wait for the dealership to open the next day.

Just across the street was a small motel. We locked the car and checked in. We'd lost money on the tow truck, wasted a full night in the motel and I could see my money going out on food, hotel and repair. I couldn't sleep.

It was a Saturday morning. As soon as the dealership opened at eight o'clock, I went right over. They looked at the car and said they'd have to replace the entire axle. They said, "You are fortunate because we have one." It took them two or three hours until they had it back together. Then I went to pick up my family. We needed to get going.

The entire town was basically built inside a circle. All the streets were one way. We left the dealership and I looked for a way to go south, but I couldn't find an exit out of the city. Finally I found a road going south. While I was searching for the way out, I looked at the dashboard and saw that a red light had come on. I thought it was just something that came with an old car and decided to ignore it. There must have been a six-miles stretch of road out of the city that went straight uphill. I could feel the car losing power. I pressed down on the gas, and the car traveled barely thirty miles an hour. Near the top of the hill, we drove a bit more, then I heard *djonn-djoon-djoon* coming from the engine and wondered what was going on.

A couple of miles later, the car died completely, right in the middle of nowhere. It was like midday, one o'clock in the afternoon. I opened the hood. It looked like an airplane; the engine was so tremendous. I saw a patrol car approach. In Mexico they are called the Green Angels. They help people in emergencies. The driver stopped and asked me what was going on. I told him the car had been making a funny noise and then it died. I tried several times to start the car, but it sounded like the engine was frozen. The battery was dead also. I was getting frustrated, worried for my family and thinking of all the money and time we were losing.

The driver said that the car probably needed a new starter. So he stopped another car headed to the village and asked the driver to take me to town for a new starter so that eventually they could replace the bad one right there on the road. I told my wife and kids to stay in the car and wait for me; it should not take too long. They were very scared about this. It was already after two o'clock in the afternoon

So the guy took me to town to look for a shop that sold a starter. It's Saturday afternoon in a small Mexican town in June. We finally found a place where I could buy the starter. But I didn't know how to install it. The shop just sold parts. The guy suggested that the best thing to do now was haul the car back here via a tow truck.

It was five o'clock by now. I could see gray clouds approaching in the gathering dark. A storm was coming up. As soon as the guy called for the tow truck, the weather broke. In Mexico, the thunderclouds are powerful. Now they were making all this thunderous noise and beginning to pour heavy rain.

The guy called the tow truck company, and the driver said, "We have another call. There's been an accident with the rain. It's going to take a while."

There was no way to communicate with my wife. It was pouring like crazy, and she was out there alone with the kids. It was getting really dark. I was worried about her, and there was no way to get to the car.

Finally the tow truck arrived, after an hour and a half. It was still raining and dark. When the truck drove me out to my car to bring it back to town, my kids and my wife were crying; she was upset, scared to death.

"Look at how you've left us!"

The guy towed us back to the village again. We went looking for a mechanic. The guy said, "Good luck. Everyone is at the bar." So we looked and looked and looked, with the car still hooked up behind.

Finally we found a shop that was open around 8:30 at night. He pulled the car over a ramp and looked inside the engine. He discovered that the oil pump wasn't working, which is what caused the engine to seize up. This was very bad news. He said we needed to replace the engine and continued by saying, "You can buy one in the United States and in a week it will be here."

What?

Next week? Are you kidding? I don't want to spend a week here! It was going to cost three thousand dollars to fix that car. No way. I told the man, "You know what? Here's the car. I don't want it. I won't spend a penny more on it."

He put the engine back together. Everything else was still inside. We went to the same hotel we were at the day before and left the car in the street at the mechanic's. The guy gave us a ride to the hotel. Again, I couldn't sleep.

What are we going to do now?

It's Sunday morning now. There's no place in the village to find a rent-a-car. There was a guy out selling vegetables, like in a little market. I asked him how far Monterrey was from here. I explained to him my situation, that I needed a small truck to haul all my belongings to Monterrey in order to rent a car there. He said it was about one hundred miles, "and if you want to wait a little bit, there's a guy coming who has a big truck with an open back for produce. You can put all your belongings there, and then we can take you to Monterrey."

I explained to my wife the plan to go to Monterey and rent-a-car using the produce truck to carry all our stuff. She was not happy with it. But there was no other way now.

The guy arrived. We went to the car and put its entire contents in the back of the open-air truck. Everything you can imagine, from clothing to kitchenware and utensils, luggage and toys; plus, on top of that, I had a dis-contructed wooden box for everything I wanted to buy in Mexico and ship to France for the decoration of the restaurant. I didn't want to waste my time in Mexico looking for wood. I'd put it in pieces on top of the car.

So we set out for Monterrey, driving eighty miles an hour along a straight road. Everything started flying away from the back. I was back there myself trying to hold everything down. My wife and kids were inside the cabin with the driver. I saw the storm clouds threatening again. By now it was four or five o'clock. I saw it was going to rain again. Everything we had was exposed in the truck.

The guy took us to a crappy hotel. He probably thought we were homeless. I said, "No way are we going to stay in a hotel like this. I saw another hotel on a hill as we were getting to Monterrey, called Ramada Inn. Let's go to that one."

The driver said, "Ooh, but it is very nice and costs much more."

"I don't care. That's where I want to stay."

We drove up the hill. We were outside the city as we climbed to the hotel. You could see the valley below. Everybody on staff wore a nice white uniform, waiting for the car to pull up. When they saw us arrive in a truck, they said, "The delivery entrance is over there."

The driver said, "It is not a delivery. It's a guest."

The valet looked at us in disbelief. "Okay."

The truck stopped at the door right in front of the hotel. I went to check in. In the meantime, the driver put everything that was in the truck onto the sidewalk. Imagine when someone is moving and everything is taken out of the boxes, every item we had in the car. The valet looked and said, "What do you want to do with all that?"

"Put it in the room, of course."

So they moved everything into the room and left it right on the floor, behind the door, in front of the bed. We couldn't even go out; there was so much stuff. I had to tip everybody. Once we were in, it was already seven thirty at night. I ordered room service dining for all of us. When the food arrived, the server could not get in. I had to step over everything to get the food. It was just a mess.

We spent the night there. The next morning I had to rent a car. It was a Monday. I went into town in a taxi which took me to a rent-a-car. I asked for the biggest car they could get. They had a Monte Carlo and an Oldsmobile that was not that big, but it was the biggest one they had.

I drove back to the hotel. There was a little window in the back of the bedroom that opened onto the parking lot about seven feet below.

I said to my wife, "Instead of going through the lobby, if you lower all the stuff from the window, I'll put it in the car."

So that's what we did. She threw everything down to me. We loaded the car all the way to the roof. The kids could hardly fit into their seats.

I said, "That's it. We're driving all the way through. We're not stopping until we get to Cuernavaca."

We left late Monday morning and drove in the rain most of the day and part of the evening. I hadn't slept well for two nights because of worry, frustration and anger.

By eight o'clock we were in Queretaro, north of Mexico City. We still had three hundred and fifty kilometers to go but had to stop because I could not drive any more; I was very tired. We found a hotel for the night and took a minimum amount of stuff into the room just to sleep. I put my passport and cash in a small handbag, which I always kept with me.

We spent the night. In the morning, we had a quick breakfast and saw that everything was okay for us to go.

As soon as we got to the car, my son said, "Daddy, I have to go to the bathroom." I put my handbag on the roof of the car so that I could open the door for my son.

Once that was taken care of, off we went. But I left my bag on the roof—money, passport, credit cards, everything.

We took the highway, which was a toll road. Along the way I realized I had not retrieved my bag.

I pulled off to the side to see that I'd lost it. Oh . . . my . . . God. I couldn't make a U-turn as the road was divided. I got out of the car and walked back for about a mile. I didn't see anything on the road. I went back to the car and said to my wife, "We've got to go to the police. We don't have any documents, money or anything."

We kept on driving until we found a U-turn and drove back to Queretaro. Once there, I went to the headquarters of the Federales and explained in my broken Spanish what happened.

They asked if I'd seen anyone on the road.

"Yeah, a truck with four or five guys shoveling gravel on the side of the road."

"Oh, they probably took it."

I saw a Federale guy in jeans and a T-shirt open a drawer, take out a big gun and place it in the back of his jeans. "Let's go," he said.

He drove with us in the car as we went back to where we'd been. We looked around as we drove and didn't see anything until we caught up with that road crew, six or eight of them, shoveling gravel onto the truck.

"Stop here," the Federale said. He asked the head guy if he'd seen anything on the road.

"No, senior."

They were humble people.

He made them empty the truck of everything, to prove they didn't have the bag in the gravel. I felt sorry for them. They looked and looked and found nothing. Then one of the guys said to the policeman, "I saw a guy just up ahead run, cross the highway and disappear. He picked up something."

Who knew where this guy was by now?

We went back to the station house and made a report. We had to cancel the credit cards. Luckily enough, I remembered two of them, which we stopped right away. I asked what to do about my passport. He said I'd have to go to the French embassy in Mexico City to tell them I lost it.

I had no money now, nothing at least to pay the toll road. The police gave us fifteen dollars, enough to pay the toll road. We finished the report and left.

Now we were about three hours from our destination. Finally, we arrived at Cuernavaca where my wife's parents and whole family were. I had to borrow money and the next day went to Mexico City to explain to the French consulate what had happened. They had to give me another passport. Here we go, more money spent. For the credit cards, I went to a bank. They issued me new ones. All the cash I had was gone.

The next day we went to the artisanal market to buy arts and crafts for the restaurant. We shopped around for two or three days and bought what we could. We got some good things. One guy sold me a painting in black with the name of the restaurant, which we could put on a wall. I had all these ideas, including glassware of different colors and clay pots for us inside, which was typical of Mexico.

I thought we should take no more than two days in Cuernavaca, but five days went by before my boxes were ready to go. We'd also lost five days on the road, with all that money unexpectedly spent. At least everything was wrapped in paper and the boxes tacked shut.

Now I had to go to Vera Cruz, on the east coast, to find the ship that would transport my two big boxes to France. I thought about renting a Volkswagen minibus with no back seat. My wife said I shouldn't go alone and suggested I take her younger brother along with me to help. He was about sixteen or seventeen. I said okay, because it was pretty far, about seven hundred kilometers across a range of mountains, up four or five thousand feet at least. It was about a fifteen-hour ride.

We started out late in the morning and decided not to stop anywhere. As soon as we got to the foothills, it started to rain. I switched on the wind-shield wipers, and they both flew off. The kid sat with the window down and tried to clear the windshield with his hand and a towel. It was already night time, in the mountains, climbing up.

There were a lot of big trucks ahead, loaded with oranges. They traveled fifteen or twenty miles an hour, max, making a terrible sound. We drove behind on a two-lane road. As soon as I could pass one of them, I'd shift into second gear. After I passed, I had to shift back into third. I drove all the way to Vera Cruz like this. The van was a piece of junk. Sometimes I felt that it was going to stall.

Finally, we got to Vera Cruz in the early morning after driving all night.

Once there, I looked for the port and ended up on a one-way street, driving the wrong way against traffic. I saw in the rearview mirror that a motorcycle cop was behind me. He looked like a cop, but he wasn't dressed the whole way. He passed and gestured for me to stop. My brother-in-law said I should pull over, but I told him to shut up; we'd keep going.

The cop got mad. He passed me again and cut me off. I stopped. He came to my driver's side window and in Spanish asked me for my papers. He wanted to know who I was and where I was going. I answered by saying that I spoke no Spanish, only English. The guy kept on in Spanish, and I kept telling him I spoke only English. I knew Spanish, but I told the guy with me not to say a word.

I told the cop I was a tourist and didn't know what he was saying.

"Okay, follow me," he ordered.

So I did until I saw he was taking us out of town. We went off onto a side road, and he stopped.

I got out of the van and walked up next to him. He asked me for money. Then, in broken Spanish, I said to him, "Do you know who I am? I am a tourist. Do you know that what you're asking is against the law? So now, know what? We are going to see your boss, together, you and I, and we are going to tell him what you just did."

"Hoh, no, no, no. Please, please."

There was nothing else he could do. He left. I got back in the van.

Finally we got to the port to do the paperwork and load the boxes. Then we drove back home to Cuernavaca. There was no rain on the way back, so we drove faster and got back late at night after twelve hours on the road. We slept in our sister-in-law's apartment in Mexico City. She had an apartment on the third floor. I parked in front so I could see the van. We went to bed and slept. In the morning, I had to give the car back. When I got up, I looked out the window at the car. All four tires were completely flat.

My God, I cannot drive like this. So we called the rental place and told them the car was dying when I put it in neutral and the windshield wipers had blown off and now the four tires are flat. It was a piece of junk. So the guy came and picked up the car and gave me a fifty per cent discount on the bill. We stayed a few more days. I had to go back to the French consulate to pick up my passport.

And now it was time to fly to France.

Restaurant Pancho Villa

We arrived in Paris, then traveled to my parents' house in Avignon. My boxes were supposed to take three weeks to arrive for me to pick up at the port of Marseilles. In the meantime, I went to the bank because, when I left Los Angeles, I'd made a wire transfer from the bank there to my bank in Avignon. The transfer included the money that would go toward the restaurant.

So when I went to the bank the next day to find that my balance was around one hundred dollars. I said, "What? I transferred around sixty thousand dollars. You're telling me I have only one hundred dollars in the account? What's going on? No way."

They said, "That's what we have."

I said, "This is ridiculous! Where's my money?"

The bank in Avignon tried to call the bank in Los Angeles. It was the same company bank, affiliated with the Bank of Paris (BNP). The Los Angeles bank insisted that they had made the transfer and that the money was supposed to be in my Avignon account. But the next day they got a call from the bank in Beverly Hills saying, "We apologize. The lady who was supposed to wire the money put it in the safe for the next day and quickly forgot to wire it."

How could stupidity like that happen? That money stayed in Beverly Hills for three weeks while I was in Mexico. Finally, it was wired to me. Right away I went to buy a pre-owned Volvo. It was a couple of years old. My wife liked Volvos. She said it would be nice to get another one. So we went to the dealership to pick up the car. It was already late in the afternoon, around five o'clock. The guy said, "Do you have insurance?"

"No, I don't."

"We'll go tomorrow; the office is already closed," he said. "Do you want to take the car now?"

I said yes and paid cash for it, planning to get insurance the next morning.

We began the drive back to my mother's house. There was a long boulevard which was unfamiliar to me, with a lot of traffic lights. It was five thirty or so. The sun was coming down close to the horizon, full blast in front of my eyes. I couldn't see, but I kept driving. I ran a red light. Boom! A car crashed into me, bashing in half of my car. And I had no insurance.

The car had hit me in the right back corner. There was a lot of damage. My wife was upset. I was upset and crying at the same time. I could not believe all this was happening to us. We were only ten kilometers—six miles—from home.

Thank God, the car was still able to run, and nothing happened to us.

We went back to my mother's house, and the next day I bought insurance and took the car to a body shop. Because it was a foreign car, the parts were more expensive. It'd take a week to repair, and the cost would be about two thousand dollars. I couldn't take it. But I had no choice but to say, "Go ahead." So I left it there.

In the meantime, we needed another car, SUV like, because every morning I would need to go to the market. So I bought an old station wagon, a Renault 6, very cheap, just to drive to the market. We used that car for a while until I could pick up the Volvo. Then we could move to Nice.

Once there, we had to find a place to stay. We said, "Let's look for an apartment." I didn't realize the rents were so expensive, so I said, "We're here. We'll have to take what we can find."

We found a place near a preschool. Cuca hadn't seen the restaurant yet. When we got to Nice, I wasn't sure where it was. We drove from the beachfront to the site, which took half an hour of driving up mountains and through canyons.

She kept saying, "Where are you going? Where are you going?"

"To the restaurant."

"I thought it would be on the beach."

"It's very expensive on the beach. I had to find one further in the backcountry."

That was another big blow to my wife. When she saw the restaurant she said, "Oh my God, it's so ugly. Why did you come all the way over here to take this place?"

"We'll make money, then we'll see."

We started to make renovations. My dad came to help. This was the middle of July1980. I hired a handyman. The boxes finally arrived from Mexico. I was happy to see what was taking place.

Once we started, I had to work on the transfer of my liquor license as it was still under the prior owner's name. There was also transfer of ownership for the business license. Then I had to have inspections from the fire department and the health department.

For the transfer of the lease, I needed a lawyer. In France it's a little different, more like a notary public. The guy who referred me to buy the restaurant knew a notary/lawyer who, he said, would take care of all my paperwork. He said he was young and just starting a business and wouldn't charge too much. I said, "Okay, that's great." I gave him all the paperwork concerning a liquor license, the transfer of the license for the restaurant and contacting the fire department. He said everything would be okay.

In the meantime, we were making modifications in the restaurant. A few days later, the fire department came to make their inspection. They said I needed to have a new fire exit and an open window for so many people.

I said, "This place has been here for twenty years. Why do I have to put in all these changes now?"

They said it was because of a new code. Nobody told me that. Now I had to spend more money on these new changes and additions. They said that, if I didn't make the changes, I could not open.

We had to do it, so we did it. The money kept going out.

Two or three weeks later, we were ready to open. We put up the sign "Pancho Villa" and bought advertising in the newspaper to announce our opening. The date was set. I also wanted to have music on the weekends, so we started talking to people. We went to a fair in Nice and saw a trio of Bolivian musicians play there. I thought they were impressive and got them to agree to play weekends for us. With them, I thought we could bring in more people.

I asked them if they knew someone else we could hire to play different kinds of performances. They knew kids from the University in Paris who were from Mexico and Argentina and different countries from South America and would be willing to play for us. That was exciting. In the meantime, I had to find a server and a dishwasher. I had my menu, and my wife dressed in a Mexican costume to be the host. We were ready to open, but I didn't have my liquor license.

I spoke to the guy who was supposed to be arranging everything. "I need my liquor license. Where is it?"

"Oh, sorry, it took a bit longer."

"I can't open like this. I need that license."

A few more days went by. Nothing. I called again. The guy told me that it was still going to take longer. This was weird. It should not have taken more than a day or two. It's been two weeks now, and I'd already paid the guy. I was not happy with that.

In the meantime, as we were renovating, I met a few people in construction. One of them was a truck driver for a transport company near the restaurant. I told him about the difficulty with my papers. He said there were a lot of Italian and Corsican mafia in that business, and the guy I was talking to was involved in the mafia, too.

He said, "This is not clear," and started to investigate the lawyer. "Come with me, and we'll look for your papers."

We went to the lawyer's apartment. He lived on the fourth or fifth floor. We rang the bell, and a lady wearing an eye shade opened the door.

"Yes? Who are you?"

We told her and asked her about the lawyer (his name was Mr. Conte).

"Oh, he is not here."

As soon as the girl said that he wasn't there, the guy who came with me forced the door open.

"What are you doing?" I said.

"Come on; let's go in."

"You can't do that."

I realized the guy was a racketeer, a mafioso, whatever. So we broke into the apartment to see the office. There were piles of papers all over the floor and his desk. It was a mess. The guy with me started looking for my papers. He searched through all the files and threw more papers on the floor. The girl started to cry. She called the police. I thought to myself, *My God, what am I going to do?*

The mafia guy was tearing through the papers and finally found my license. Nothing had been done after the lawyer took my money. As soon as we were ready to go, he looked out the window and saw that the cops were arriving. He said, "Let's wait for the police."

The cops came up and into the apartment. One was a detective in civilian clothes, and the other was in uniform.

The detective looked at the guy who had taken me there and said, "Oh, you again? What's going on with you, man? Every time we have a problem, you're present."

The mafioso told about the lawyer and what he did and showed the papers strewn all over. The cops looked at me. "Who are you?"

I told the cops about opening my restaurant, paying the guy for my license, and how he never got back to me.

"Do you have a paper with you? A license? Identification?"

I gave him my California driver's license. He said, "What is that?"

I explained that I was just in from California and didn't have my French identification yet. He looked at me and said, "So what are you going to do?"

"I just want my license. We found it, so we're going to get going."

"Okay, so get out of here."

We left with my liquor license, and I went back to my restaurant. I told my wife what had happened and that we needed someone else to do the transfer because we could be in trouble.

On the same night, the phone rang. The restaurant wasn't open. The guy on the phone said he wanted to speak to Frederic Castan. He said he was the uncle of Mr. Conte, the lawyer. His voice was very deep. He asked about what had happened. I said that what his nephew did was very bad. He agreed with me, but I got scared because I knew these people never leave you alone.

I hung up the phone. I didn't want to deal with these guys anymore. I didn't want more problems. I didn't say anything to my wife about this.

The next day I had to find someone else to process my license application. We also had to hire someone to refurbish the door and window so we could open the restaurant. I was getting very tired. A few days later, we finally opened the Pancho Villa restaurant with a small reception. It was crazy. I was the only cook, and I had to go to the market every morning very early and buy all the produce, fish, meat, and dairy for my menu.

So I did. Luckily, across the road, they were building a huge bridge for the toll road. It was something like three or four hundred feet high. There were about 100 guys working on that project, so of course when I opened the door at seven o'clock in the morning, they started coming in for coffee and croissants. That meant a little business for us before I went into the kitchen to prepare for lunch and dinner. My wife had to get the kids ready for school, so she couldn't get in until ten o'clock. She helped me a little bit. Then I hired a dishwasher, a lady from Morocco.

I had to find a server, which was very difficult because Nice, being a city that had seasonal tourism, affords a lot of money for servers in high season. Restaurants are busy, and their prices are high. Then, when the restaurants close in October, the servers go on unemployment and make ninety percent of what they had been making.

Opening a restaurant that operated all year long, I couldn't afford to pay a server that amount of money. No way. I don't make enough myself.

But a server came to me and said, "I'll work for you if you pay me cash and don't declare me. I can still get unemployment."

I didn't have a choice, so I agreed. He came to work, and every week I had to give him cash.

Time went by. Every day he stole money from the cash register. And he was getting drunk. He wore a Mexican costume we brought, with a hat, because it was a Mexican restaurant.

For dinner, we added candles to the table settings. One night while I was in the kitchen, the server had a table of four. One of the diners was a famous singer who had retired. They ordered a bottle of wine, then a second bottle. The server, who was already drunk, said, "I'm not going to give you the second bottle." In saying so, as he was leaning over the table, one of the strings in his hat dipped into the candle's flame and caught fire.

The guests stood up and started to yell at the server. My wife quickly called me out of the kitchen. When I came out front, they said they were leaving. I apologized to the server and bought them dinner. The singer was upset, but he was laughing too. I went back into the kitchen. They were the only guests that night. I told my wife that this was all beyond what I could imagine. We started to argue. It was already late, maybe around twelve o'clock. So we closed and left to go home.

We had a babysitter who came at five o'clock so we could be free to work at the restaurant. My older son was only four; my other son was one. The babysitter expected us home by ten thirty at night. Because of the incident at the restaurant, it was after eleven thirty before we got home. We lived a few miles from the restaurant. Our apartment was on the second floor, with a balcony. As we drove home, the window was open and we could hear a cry. We looked up and saw our older son on the balcony rail, crying.

We stopped the car and ran up to the apartment. I was sweating, scared, crying, "What's going on?"

Because we had not arrived on time, the babysitter left and left the kids alone. Georges was crying his lungs out on the balcony.

On top of everything else, my wife declared that she'd had enough, "I can't handle this anymore."

So many problems, left and right. I kept thinking, *What do I do now? I can't give all this up. I've put everything into it. I have nothing left. I owe money everywhere, to the bank, the contractor, the insurance company . . . What do I do? I'm sorry, but we've got to keep going.*

One day a couple of guys came into the bar and asked if I needed protection. I did not understand. What kind of protection? Well, the guys said, "If some mafia goons come and ransack the place, we could be your defense." I told them, that "I don't need any of that. Everything will be fine." They left.

Every morning at five, I went to the market to buy my produce, my fish, whatever I needed for the day. I had limited cash to pay, because everything was COD. I'd go back to the restaurant at eight to prepare breakfast, lunch, and dinner. We'd close at ten. On weekends, when we had music, we'd stay open until midnight. I was getting only about five hours of sleep a night.

Time went by. I was dealing with more problems. My wife and I weren't talking. She was hanging with all the guys because she needed someone to talk to. I was getting sick, to the point where I had a constant headache. I called a doctor who came to the restaurant to see me.

He said, "Sir, you don't eat. You smoke a pack a day. You drink ten or twelve espressos a day. Your body has limitations. That's why your brain is protesting."

My weight was down to one-hundred-and-forty pounds. I was a skeleton. A nurse would come in to give me injections of nutrients, just so I could keep going.

I did that every day, for a year, no days off. From Mondays through Thursdays, the cuisine was mostly bistro style. On weekends, I did Mexican. Business was slow, because the restaurant's location was far from the center of Nice; also, we lacked advertisement.

I didn't want to throw food away, so I changed the menu a bit. I served a margarita pitcher with Smirnoff vodka; I couldn't find tequila in France. I'd put a pitcher of a margarita with ice on the table; people would order it without knowing the difference. They loved it.

I was making sixty to eighty covers a night on weekends, but it wasn't enough to pay the bills. Other things I had to pay, besides the staff, were social security, plus a government fee for health care, and unemployment insurance. Ninety percent of the salary you paid to an employee went to the government. If you paid ten dollars an hour, nine went to the government.

That was a lot of money going out. Plus, I was backing up on my bills. The money was going, going, going. And I had to pay the musicians. Beside that, I had stereo music for the rest of the weekdays. I had to pay for the rights to that music. Sasem, it's called, another tax on entertainment and music, whether it's live or not. Nobody had told me about this. I received a bill. *What is this?* I'd already been in operation for three or four months. The bill was enormous. I said, "Forget it. I don't have the money for this now." So I didn't pay for it. The important thing was to keep going, keep going. We needed to survive.

But I was getting sicker and sicker.

One weekend night about a year later, three guys came in at ten o'clock. They went to the bar and asked for one round of drinks, then another. Then they moved to a table next to the bar. It was already eleven thirty, quarter to twelve. They said they wanted to eat. People were already leaving. We were closing. I said, "Let me see what I can prepare for you guys."

I went back in the kitchen and fixed something quick and brought the meal out to them at the table. They ordered champagne. By then everyone was gone. I opened the bottle of champagne. They drank it and ate the food I gave them. At quarter to one, they ordered another bottle. I could not say no because it's money, right? The drinks at the bar, the food, the champagne. So I brought another bottle. It's one thirty already. By law we're supposed to close by then.

They asked for another bottle. I said, "Sorry, guys, we're closed. We're tired. I've been up since five in the morning and have to open tomorrow morning again. We need to ask you to leave."

By now they were drunk. They wanted to continue. So I opened another bottle. Now it was two o'clock, two fifteen. I said to my wife, "What are we going to do?"

Finally I said to the guys, "That's it. We cannot do any more. You've got to leave now."

One of them looked at me and said, "Why don't you put us out?"

"I don't want to put you out, butcas you can see, we're closed."

They didn't want to leave. I told my wife to shut off the music and the lights. As soon as she started to shut off the lights, one guy stood, picked up the table with all the glasses and dishes on it, and threw it across the room.

I cried, "What are you doing?'

"Shut up," he said, and boom! He punched me in the face. I almost went down to the floor. I started to bleed from my ear. I yelled at them to stop. Another guy took my wife and pushed her against one of the big speakers at the end of the bar. I didn't know what to do. I went to the back of the bar to grab a machete and started swinging it in front of me. I said, "Whoever gets close to me I'll slash his throat!" I didn't care. I was hysterical. Remember, I was only a hundred and forty pounds. I had no power.

While I was swinging the machete, another guy was breaking everything—everything. Glasses, stereo, tables, chairs—you name it. The guy I had the altercation with must have had a knife. My mother had given me a leather jacket which I was wearing. Later I saw that it had been slashed to pieces.

They broke everything. It was now two thirty, three in the morning. They left. There was just the dishwasher, my wife and I. It was quiet.

What is going on? What do we do? My God.

The only thing to do was to call the police. This is an example of how things are Nice. I called and explained in detail everything that had happened. They said, "You are breaking the law. Look at what time it is. You should not have been open this late. It's your problem."

They hung up the phone.

I couldn't believe it. I just couldn't believe it. Those people almost killed me. They destroyed everything. And now the police are telling me that it's my fault? Oh man, this was out of this world!

We locked the door and went home. I couldn't sleep. In the little bit that was left of the night, I kept thinking, *What am I going to do?* I didn't have the money to go anywhere else. No cash, nothing. I had to find a way to do something.

But this is tenacity. This is not giving up.

In the morning I went back. I had it in my mind: I cannot give up. I returned with my dishwasher. My wife didn't come. She stayed with the kids. I did what I could to put everything back together.

I know it was the mafia who came. I recalled the day two or three months after opening when those two guys came to me and said, "If you want protection, we are here to protect you. We can put a machine in here for gaming so you can make money. We'd be here to protect you because you never know what could happen. Every month you can pay us some money."

I said to them, "Why do I need protection? I'm okay. I don't want to owe anything to anybody. I'm fine."

"Well, think about it."

"Okay."

A month or two later, they came back. "Are you sure? There are a lot of things happening. People are losing their businesses because of racketeering and violence."

I said, "I'm okay. I'm alright. Thank you very much for your help anyway."

They left.

Those were the same people, the same mafia people, who came to break everything in my place, not the same physically but the same group.

The next day I cleaned up the restaurant and opened for business as best I could.

I called the gendarmerie. When I was in Mexico, I met one of the guards at the French Embassy. We became friends. He said to me, "I'm going back to France to become commandant of the gendarmerie in La Napoule." (La Napoule is a small village near Nice.)

So I remembered that guy. It had been almost a year. I called the gendarmerie in La Napoule and asked for him. He came to the phone and said, "Hey, how are you doing?"

I explained to him what happened. "What can I do? This is ridiculous." He explained to me that the gendarmerie and the police are two different things. The police serve the city. The gendarmes are not allowed to interfere. But if I told him more, where those guys were—I knew one of them worked for the trucking company, in the same mafia clan as the guy who took me to get my papers—he would confront them in his uniform and scare them into staying away from my place.

That's what he did. The next day he went and told them never to go back to my restaurant or even try anything, because then they'd have to deal with him personally.

There were a couple of middle-aged married couples who came in every Sunday morning at nine o'clock for coffee at the bar. I explained what had happened. One hour later, a guy came in, maybe 5'6", built like a square. He came up to the bar, looked at me, and said, "I need to talk to you."

"Okay. Tell me what you want to tell me."

The couples were there, so I didn't feel alone.

But the guy said, "No, no, no, no, no. Come walk with me."

"Tell me what you have to tell me here."

The guy refused again, so I told my guests I'd be back, watch the bar for me for a minute.

The guy took me to the bathroom. He closed the door and locked it from the back. We were alone. I was taller than him, almost by a head. He grabbed me by the shirt, looked me in the eye, and said, "Tell your friend, the gendarme, to forget about this and leave us in peace, because you will pay with your kids. Understand me?"

He left. I went back to the bar and told the people what he had said. They said, "This is unbelievable."

I told them, "That's it. I cannot do this anymore. I got to get out of here. I have no money, but I've got to get out for the safety of my family."

The Great Escape

There was another customer who was in the wood business and came in once or twice a week. We became good friends. I told him I needed some help. "Can you buy my car? Whatever you want to give me is okay. I've only had it for a year and a half."

He offered half of its value. I accepted. He gave me the cash, and I promised him the car in a week.

I had the other car I used for the market, the old station wagon. I needed more money. I didn't have enough to buy us plane tickets to go back to Mexico. I couldn't go back to the States because by now my Green Card had expired.

I had an idea how to collect more cash to leave Nice as quickly as possible. I called close friends and clients from the restaurant and proposed that they buy all my decorations and the entire Pancho Villa inventory of booze and wine, for cash only, at bargain prices.

The same weekend about 40 people came. I had a big display for them to pick and choose what they liked. Everything was sold in an hour.

Now I had enough to buy plane tickets to Mexico City, via Paris and Madrid. I had a small amount of cash for later. Then I had to think about how I could transport all our belongings in two suitcases.

I put together the wooden box I'd kept from Mexico, loaded it with personal items, mainly pictures, paintings, and family souvenirs, and took it to the harbor in Nice to ship to my sister-in-law in LA.

I put all my bills in a big envelope and sent it to my bookkeeper with a note saying that we were leaving due to unforeseen circumstances. "Please take care of those bills and call or write to all our creditors." That was it. By the time he received it, we'd be gone.

I closed the restaurant and put up a big sign. This was the end of May or early June. It said, "Closed for Annual Vacation" (kind of weird at the beginning of summer, in this very seasonal city).

We took the old car, the station wagon, the two suitcases, and caught the eight o'clock morning flight to Paris and stayed overnight for the next flight. At the Nice airport, I left the station wagon with the key in it. If somebody wanted to take it, that was okay with me.

My wife was angry. I carried the suitcases, which didn't have wheels. They were close to forty pounds each. It was a long way. We didn't have money for a taxi, so we walked to an airport hotel, in the heat, with the kids crying. At the hotel we slept, got up the next morning, and took the bus to the airport.

At Madrid, we had to change planes. My mom, who had passed away, had bought me a beautiful watch as my high school graduation gift. The band needed repair. When she came to L.A. to see my son for the first time, I gave it to her to have it fixed in France, telling her I'd pick it up when we visited her there. In the meantime, she passed away before she could replace the band. I picked it up when we opened the restaurant and had it in my pocket when we changed planes in Madrid. It fell out, and I didn't notice until we got to Mexico. It was the only thing left I had by which to remember her.

We arrived in Mexico City after a sixteen-hour flight and went to pick up our suitcases. We waited and waited and waited while all the other people picked up their suitcases, until ours arrived, the very last of the last. One of them had broken open. Everything was falling out. It was an old suitcase. We put back the clothes.

Earlier, my wife had called her sister from France to tell her we were returning to Mexico. Everything had been in limbo then; we hadn't even purchased our plane tickets yet. Cuca's brother-in-law came to the airport in

Mexico City to pick us up. He took over two hours. There was a lot of traffic. By then, the kids were already tired and crying.

He took us to his house and gave us one bedroom. The kids could sleep with their cousins.

That was it. We began to start our new life.

I knew I couldn't get back into the United States because my Green Card had expired. The original plan was to reach the border by car and cross illegally. If I said I'd traveled to Tijuana from the US that morning and was now coming back, there was no way they could check. They just wave you through if you're coming from the San Diego side, as long as we have our passports and the Green Card. They'll check if you're coming in from Mexico by plane, but by car they can't tell when you've made your first crossing.

But we didn't have any money. If I were to go back to L.A., where could we stay? I needed to make a little before we could go. We had two kids. If I were to go by myself, I could find a place to sleep. But with kids and a wife, it's different.

I thought it would be safer for us to stay with my wife's family in Mexico where I could try and find a job and earn enough to go to the United States. That was the idea. But when we got to Mexico City, I didn't have a job and didn't speak Spanish. So here we were. After a few days, I had to start knocking on doors to see if I could work somewhere. I went to big hotels, and I spoke English. Most of the management speaks English in those large international hotels. And most of those managers came from Europe.

After many attempts, I found nothing. Then in one of them, I met a French food and beverage director named Francis Seguin. He was a director for a big hotel called Camino Real, which belonged to the Westin company. I asked him if he had any jobs as a cook or sous-chef. He said they didn't have anything then, but he had an American friend who had two restaurants, one well known in Mexico City, that might need some help.

He gave me the name and address so I went to the restaurant there whose owner's name was Borzani. His son, who ran the place, was called

Jimmy. It was a very expensive place. A lot of politicians went there. The service was very well orchestrated. They did table-side service, including carving and flambé, like in France. You needed to wear a tie to get in.

I went to the restaurant and asked for Mr. Borzani. We sat down. He spoke English. His father was Hungarian, but Jimmy had been born in the United States and was married to an American girl.

He said, "I have one of the best restaurants in Acapulco, and I need somebody who will help me in the kitchen because it's a disaster, and also to oversee the service because the guy I had there left. I need someone strong to manage all this, with a great culinary background and a capacity for leadership."

Another challenge was there for me. I said, "Okay, no problem." He informed me that it was an Italian restaurant. I replied that there is nothing I cannot do.

Acapulco is a six-hour drive from Mexico City, about 350 kilometers. This was before the era of toll roads. You have to cross over the mountains before you can get to the coast, and you can't drive faster than forty-five to 60 miles an hour.

He told me he'd expect to meet at the restaurant at a certain time and day, and they would provide an apartment for me and a car. During the season, from November fifteenth to about the end of April, you were expected to work seven days a week. After that, you could take two days a week off.

I agreed. I needed a job. The money was not a big deal, but I didn't have to pay rent and I would have a car. I told my wife to come over. We had a place to stay, a little house; it'll be easy for us. My father-in-law loaned me some money, maybe five hundred dollars, to start my life in Acapulco. We rented a car to get there and stayed at the hotel for a couple of weeks, in an apartment suite with a kitchen and two bedrooms.

We were living well, near the oceanside. I went to the restaurant and was introduced to the director who didn't have a clue about what was going on. The owner was with me. He expected a new menu and a revamped service. It was a big place.

So here we were. We had been in Mexico City for four months before I could get a job. Now I had to shine. I thought a lot about how to bring authentic Italian food to Acapulco, with local ingredients. When we arrived, I went right away to see the restaurant. I was stunned. All the seating was outside. There was a huge patio dining space, about three hundred and fifty seats, under large palm trees, with a fountain in the middle. It was beautiful, one of the top restaurants at the time, called Villa Demos. Demos was the name of the partner to the American. He was Italian, a very good chef, but he had died three years before I got there. Then they used the guy who didn't know how to run the place.

First, I revamped the menu, introducing different pasta made fresh with semolina and local seafood. The big task was to retrain the cooks. I had to deal with the union in Mexico, and of course when the summer came, I saw that their skills were lacking and they were reluctant to change. One day one of them came in so drunk he couldn't stand up. I told him to go home. He complained to what they call the syndicato (union). A delegation from the syndicato came the next day and wanted to put me out of the country. The boss of the hotel paid the union to keep quiet.

The season started in November and kept us busy through April. People waited for up to forty-five minutes to be seated, and we had three hundred and fifty seats. I wanted to establish the action on the floor of the patio, so I created several stations where servers did flambee consisting of different salads with the dressing done in front of the guests like, for example, spinach salad with hot bacon cooked right there at the table, with the veal and pasta.

We worked at an unbelievable pace. I had eighty-five servers and busboys. The patio had twenty stations, and each station had about four tables. We did an average of one-and-a-half seatings a night. When the patio was full, it was a show of its own and it could be very fairly splendid to see all the action—the mixing of fettuccine alfredo, spaghetti puttanesca, linguine al vongole, crepes suzette, or cherry jubilee being flambeed. And the smell! Guests grew more hungry as the evening wore on.

Mr. Borzani came in one or twice a month to check the books and eat there. He was happy with all the changes and the quality of the food.

After a month or so, I looked at the produce we were getting every day. It was a disaster. The quality was bad. The lettuce that came by truck in the morning arrived almost cooked from the heat. The avocados were mushy and almost black. Everything was terrible.

I said, "How can this be?" And the prices!

I went to the market myself. I walked around and saw the prices and the product—good products. I also realized that the profit that the delivery truck was making was enormous. So I called the boss and told him we needed to change that. We needed to go to the market to buy our own product, and the quality would be one hundred percent better. I told him we'd save money. He said, "If you think this is a good idea, go ahead."

So he bought me a truck, an old truck with the name of the restaurant on it. Every morning at five o'clock, I went to the market. It reminded me again of my Provence boyhood. I was like a kid in a toy store. I found more than I could imagine, vegetables and fruits that I had never seen before.

I shopped with a big list. Every transaction was in cash. I didn't know what three or four hundred dollars in my pocket meant in Mexico then. I'd give the guy who came with me two or three dollars, and he'd helped me carry everything. It was so much better. I even created my little produce business, selling to a couple of other small restaurants. Everyone ended up winning, buying better products at a better price. And I made money on the side.

When I went to the market in the morning, I couldn't find parking. The traffic was a mess, with trucks coming in from all over bringing their produce and live animals, plus people from farms and mountains coming in to shop.

I didn't want to park two miles away because I had to load, so I parked the truck on a double line in the street in front of the market because there was a line of cars there just to pick up the food.

After a couple of times of doing that, I found a piece of paper on my windshield and my license plate removed by the police. I had to go to the police station to pay a fine. I didn't know where it was. The guy who loaded my truck said, "I'll take you there." He did, and I had to pay to get my license plate back. I explained to the police that there was no parking; what did they expect a person to do? The officer didn't care. So I went and talked to the chief of police in Acapulco. He asked about me and where I was working. He knew about the restaurant and was impressed.

He said, "You buy me dinner when I come in with my girlfriend once in a while, and we'll forget about holding your license plate."

I said, "You've got a deal."

So I parked again in the morning, and bingo, my license plate goes. I went back to the station. I explained the deal I'd made with the chief. They said that was between him and me; they still had to take the plate. But each day, they took it and gave it back to me when I checked in. This didn't happen every day, maybe once a week. The chief was married, but he came in with a new girlfriend every time.

That was definitely another kind of life in Mexico, and I could see how much corruption there was.

Here's a True Story

We had a big round table in the middle of the restaurant. It could seat sixteen people at once. Also, we had two cabanas in the corners that were like private dining rooms that seated ten each. People from all over came in, Canadians, Americans, Europeans, friends getting together because it was private. The servers got big tips. Everyone was happy.

One day we had a reservation for sixteen people, Americans. We seated them early, by eight o'clock. Maybe a half hour later, we had a phone call from Carmen Portillo. Carmen was the wife of Mexican President Portillo. This was '81,'82. She made a dinner reservation for eight. They would arrive about nine o'clock, nine thirty. I reserved one of the private cabanas for them. The Americans in the middle were eating and drinking. They were good customers, spending a good amount of money.

She arrived with six or seven people. At the entrance of the restaurant was the lounge with a bar, then a huge fountain and a very large staircase going down the patio where our guests were dining. You could see the entire restaurant from above.

When she arrived, she told the maître d', "I want the table in the middle."

He said, "I'm sorry, but there are people eating there. They're good customers. We already have a table reserved for you in a private cabin, in the corner."

"NO. NO! I don't want the corner. I want the one in the center."

"We cannot fit sixteen people in that cabana. It only seats eight. I cannot tell the people who are in the middle of their dinner to get out. They've already spent three or four bottles of Dom Perignon and expensive wine."

She grew very upset. Short story—she said, "Okay, we're leaving." So she left, saying, "You're going to hear from me."

The next night, two guys came in, and the maître d' seated them at a table for two. Maybe fifteen minutes later, two other guys came in and asked for a table. It was about 9:30, and the restaurant was full. One of the two men from the first group stood up to go to the restroom. He walked by the two other guys and fell over their table. They started to argue and got into a fistfight, all four of them, after the guy at the first table came over to defend his buddy.

One of them pulled a gun and started to fire. Ninety-six or ninety-eight bullets were fired. With shooting and reloading from four guys, this went on for twenty minutes. Thank God, nobody died. Two were injured. One Canadian had burns from bullets that grazed his skin above an ear. The bartender was above and ducked into a hole behind the bar, laying flat on his stomach. One of the bullets ricocheted off an iron door above and hit him in the kidney. He had to be taken to the hospital for surgery. There was shooting for twenty minutes.

No police came. We found out later that the shooters and Portillo's wife had a relationship.

In the meantime, with people running and screaming all over the place, the four shooters threw bags of money and marijuana that scattered all over the place. As soon as they left, the police arrived, about two dozen cops in Jeeps. They closed all access to the restaurant and held two people to interview. I was hiding in the kitchen, in the back. The investigation included questioning why there was money and marijuana all over the place. They blamed the restaurant for dealing drugs. That's really what had happened—a bad drug deal. But it was all set and orchestrated by Carmen Portillo after not being seated at the table, said, "You will hear from me."

We closed the restaurant for a week and had to pay a big amount of money to reopen. We had to fix everything that had been damaged. In the end, the police found ninety-six bullets, most of them in the palm trees and in the walls, some outside the restaurant.

We opened again for business like nothing had happened. Mr. Borzani didn't complain. He knew that's the way things are in Mexico, especially after the chief of police arranged to bring his girlfriend in to eat and drink for free. El Negro Durazo was his name. He was dealing arms and drugs. Something that struck me was that the government gave him money daily to fill up every patrol car with gas. He told his policemen to fill only fifty percent of the tank and pocketed the difference. When the patrol cars ran out of gas, the cops could go home. He did the same thing for uniforms. They gave him money for uniforms, but I never saw a cop in full uniform. One has pants only. One has only a jacket. One has a cap. Durazo was pocketing all the money. He took a piece of every policeman's pay check for what he told them was a retirement apartment. But when they retired, they received nothing. That was another form of revenue he kept for himself. We're talking about big-time money. They caught him and put him in jail, and then he died. El Negro Durazo was the chief of police in Mexico City from 1976 to 1982.

Life in Mexico was like that for me, seven days a week beginning at five o'clock in the morning with a trip to the market, back to the restaurant to prep for the day with the other guys, and then set up early afternoon in the restaurant to make sure everything was okay, and then helping the guy in the office do the payroll. This went all the way to 11:30 at night until we closed at midnight. We served the last customer at 10:30. In Mexico, people tend to eat late.

Once in a while my wife went to visit her sister. The kids started to go to school in Acapulco. After a year in France, they spoke only French. For them it was a learning curve for the first six months. But then they caught on pretty quickly.

We lived like this for three years. Being busy at the restaurant the way I was didn't help our relationship. I was saving a bit of money, so that was good. But my wife was miserable and said life here was too disorganized. "The schools—forget it. We can't raise the kids here. If you want to stay,'" she said, stay by yourself. I'm going back to the States." We started to argue. Even though she was born in Mexico, there was nothing for her there. She saw how much better it was in the United States. Her concern was mainly for the kids. For myself, I became good friends with the CPA for the restaurant. He was the godfather of my son. In Mexico, with this relationship you become "compadre." He was like family. He had his own practice; before that, he was controller for the state of Guerrero. He was high in the political hierarchy. When he retired, he still kept two bodyguards around him.

He was wealthy and well known in Acapulco. Anywhere I went with him, they gave the red-carpet treatment. If there were one hundred people waiting in line to get into the discotheque, he just walked to the head of the line, and they let him right in.

He said to me one time, "Why don't you stay here and we'll open a restaurant."

I thought it was a great idea, but when I mentioned it to my wife, she said, "No way."

After six months of arguing with her, I went to my colleague and said, "We're going back to the States." She would have gone back without me and let the marriage go. We were in bad shape together because, even though we were doing well in Acapulco, we had had such a bad time in France that it became a big turn in our lives. She hadn't forgiven me for that. I had pushed her to go with me.

She was not happy at all. She said, "I'm going to go. If you want to stay, then stay."

In the meantime, I talked to my boss, the owner of the restaurant. I told him that, after the season, we were going back to the States because my wife didn't want to stay here. He said, "Let me see what I can do. I have a plan to open a restaurant in Austin, Texas." He said the city was ready to boom, and there were plans to open a Disneyland there in the next three years.

"The market is very hot. I'm going to invest money in a restaurant there. I'm already looking at a place. Give me a couple of months, and I'll give you more information. Then, if you want, you can open the restaurant for me."

The Lone Star State

*O*n June of '85 we went to Austin, Texas.

I'd told my wife about this opportunity to go back to the States and open a new restaurant about thirty-five miles from Austin in Lago Vista, on Lake Travis. It would be called Bootlegger. She said okay. In Acapulco the season would finish at the end of April, and we'd need until the end of May to get everything cleaned up.

The only way to reenter the U.S. was by driving. I couldn't get back to the States legally, being away for almost five years. My Green Card was technically discontinued. All they had to do at customs was look at my passport to deny me entry. That's why we couldn't go by plane. My boss thought the town of Lago Vista would be a good place to invest in, so he bought some property there, including a restaurant and a house. He said that if I came in with him, I could operate the restaurant.

So we took the car we had, a station wagon, and set out for Austin with the kids. After a couple of days, we arrived at the US border where Mr. Borzani was waiting for us in a car. We had no problems crossing. I still had my Green Card. Customs didn't ask when we had last crossed.

Mr. Borzani rented a house for us in Austin where we could stay for a few months. He knew I didn't have much money. When I exchanged my Mexican pesos for American dollars, I got peanuts—three thousand dollars. I had to buy a used car; the old one was registered in Mexico and had a Mexican license. Someone else took it back for us. We bought a used Chevrolet Monte Carlo.

Texas was new to me. We finally arrived in Lago Vista, in the countryside, thirty-five miles away from Austin. We lived in a house that was only a mile from the restaurant. My wife felt better, being in the States, seeing the schools, living the way she used to. The kids didn't speak English at all, so they had to adapt again. It was hard for them. They had no friends, no communications.

There was only one mattress in the house, no furniture, and of course I couldn't buy any. There were no tables, no chairs, and no refrigerator in the kitchen. I had less than a thousand dollars left after buying the car. My boss took me to a store to buy a refrigerator. He was a guarantor to the sales contract. I put one hundred dollars into a down payment. For some reason, by the grace of God, I never received another bill. So we got the refrigerator almost for free. That was another experience from God. Even though at that time I was ignoring him, he never let me down. He was always there to hold and help me.

Mr. Borzani took me to see the Bootleggers. The deal wasn't finalized yet. He still had to finish the transfer of the license. When I saw the restaurant for the first time, I said, "My gosh." It was in the middle of the woods. It looked like a big wood cabana that could seat maybe fifty people, surrounded by pine trees. On the menu was chicken fried steak and other local specialties. I said to myself, "My God, what are we doing with this place? Who's going to come here?"

There was a local who said he was a chef who had been there and wanted to work for us. He was Texan and a very nice guy. So we got together and created a menu, keeping in count the area and clientele we would get. Chicken fried steak definitely remained on the menu. I added some Tex Mex ideas and nice BBQ dishes, nothing one would connect with my Provence style. This was another learning curve. I asked how many lunch customers they had. Twenty, maybe thirty. The nights were slow, maybe five to ten people. Disneyland wasn't coming in after all, but there was a big project in development, like Six Flags. A lot of people were investing money. The boss was looking five years ahead. He didn't see what was happening now. In the meantime, we had to survive and make the best of it.

Another thing that was bad: we had a septic tank instead of a sewer system. We had to call the pump truck twice a day when it was normal for the truck to come once a week. The toilet, the sink, the washing machine, everything flowed into the same place, and it smelled. It was terrible and cost a lot of money.

On the first weekend, a lot of bikers arrived, up to twenty. I was scared. There was even a live band that performed outside the restaurant and brought their own alcohol. I thought, *Jesus, this is going to be a touchy operation.* They got into fights and threw empty bottles out onto the street. They weren't allowed to come inside because of our license.

The owner went back to Mexico and left me with the restaurant. It was a little scary at first. I didn't know if we could make it once I saw the bills we had to pay each month. Just to drain the septic tank cost four hundred dollars a trip. We were spending eighteen hundred dollars a day, including utilities, food and liquor costs, payroll, and much more. How were we going to make it?

A month went by before the boss came back. We sat down for a meeting. I told him we had to do advertising. We were losing money left and right. At the end of one month, he'd lost fifteen thousand dollars.

He caved. He realized that the development of Six Flags would take years. After four months of operation, at the end of the summer, he made the decision to close the restaurant. I still had the house he was renting for me and my salary of three thousand dollars a month. But after he closed, that was it. I asked my wife about what we would do. Now I had no job and we were living nowhere, in the countryside, with little savings.

I had to go to Austin to look for a job. I took the car and drove thirty-five miles. Here, traffic was almost door to door. I looked for a job like a homeless person. On the third day, in a small restaurant, the owner said to me, "If you want to be a breakfast cook, we're pretty busy. I need one." He offered me the job at six-fifty an hour.

To arrive at five in the morning, I had to leave my house at four. We had only one month more where we could stay at that house, so I was running back and forth. The owner of the restaurant, who was also the chef, saw how I worked and asked me if I'd be willing to create some daily specials for lunch. I said not for the same amount of money. So he gave me a little more, nine dollars an hour. I worked on lunch and trained other cooks. But I had to find something else. There was no way I could go on making this amount of money.

After one month went by, we could no longer stay in that house. We needed to move. We didn't even have furniture, so when the time came, that part of it was easy. I had saved money by not having to pay rent, so I said, "Let's see what we can rent." We found something on the outskirts of Austin, a little two-bedroom townhome, for six hundred dollars a month. We still had an Astro van at the old restaurant, the Bootlegger. The restaurant owner, who wound up going back to Mexico, had been nice to me and said I could take it. If I could make the monthly payment, it was mine to keep. So now we had it as a second car. My wife wasn't working, so she was able to use it to take the kids to school.

As a parent, a chef's life is very demanding with long hours—sixty, seventy-plus hours a week—plus holidays and weekends. It's not a family life. A typical family life means spending time with the kids at night, helping them do homework. I used to work with them until nine or ten o'clock a night after I came home from work. On the weekend it's the same, and when they have activities at school, like sports, or shows, or show and tell, it's nice for the parents to be there for the kids and support them.

I never really could do that or only do it rarely. So my kids really missed that. They didn't have their dad's support. And my wife even more—she had to be both parents. It was more of a struggle for her. Through the kids' youth, it was sporadic to have time together. The same thing with vacations. When I had a vacation, school was in session, so we couldn't go out. Summers were busy for me. I had to work. So the only time we could take vacations was in January. So it was a hardship for them. It was the same for my wife. There were times when the marriage was very much in jeopardy.

The toughest part of the road to the present was when I decided to open a restaurant in France and take her and the kids. I spent twenty hours a day getting that place up and then losing everything. For a wife it's very difficult, because she's looking for security. Maybe not so much now, but at the time it was very important. When we wound up losing the business, the house and the cars, and winding up with no job and three hundred dollars in our pocket, and two kids, that really puts you to the test. It was the lowest moment of my life.

That's why the marriage suffered. It was rocky for the next ten years. But I like to think that things will get better. I believe in God. That's helped me a lot to survive those tough times. There was a point where I went away from church and God. I became lost. But my roots helped me stand up instead of falling down and giving up completely.

In Austin one day, all this hit me. After I lost the restaurant in France, we lived in Mexico for three-and-a-half years before moving to Texas. One day I got a call. I was walking in front of a church. The doors were open. At first I merely stood there. Then I heard a voice saying, "I am here; don't forget about me. Why did you run away?" God spoke to me. I went into the church and began to pray. Tears started to run down my cheeks, and I asked for forgiveness. That began a big change in my life. I had separated from my wife and went to live by myself. I left the townhouse where we lived and found an apartment.

It became a time of reflection for me. I kept working, but that day in church made me realize how much I missed my wife and kids. I laid [everything?] down on the floor and asked, "What am I doing?" By then we'd been separated for nearly a month. It was a difficult time for me; her too. She felt terrible. I'd left her because she was so mad at me, going back to the time where we lost everything. I couldn't endure it. I couldn't handle it. It was my fault, I know. She was angry and couldn't forgive what I did. She became cold. She criticized everything I did. She wouldn't speak to me.

That day when I went to church became a turning point. I would go back to pick up the kids once in a while, whenever I could. On one of those days, I asked her to forgive me for what I did. I really wished with all my heart to come back home. "I'll try my best to be a better man and a better husband." It was difficult for her to take me back. It took a few days. The day she accepted, I still knew I would have had to put in a lot of effort to fix it and to show her I really wanted to be together. But—talking about my wife—when you've been stuck very badly so many times, that for her the scar was very deep.

It took a lot of time. It still isn't what it was before. But we've come a long way. My being busy all the time didn't help with the kids. It took its toll on the marriage.

So it takes a lot of sacrifice and effort to make it happen. Not to give up when it becomes very difficult is crucial. I kept working and went back home to support my family. I could have moved out and kept going, but no, I focused on family. That was a sacrifice. When you work sixty or seventy hours a week, you know that's tough. But I made it, and I don't complain. We survived; we went up the hills again. When you look around the industry of being a chef, you see that sixty per cent are divorced. It's very rare to see a chef who has stayed married since the beginning of his career. When I talk to chefs, most of them are separated, divorced, or remarried two or three times. I put my wife to the test many times, but she accepted the conditions. She continued to support me.

She's very smart. There are many times when she gave me good advice and I didn't take it. My ego got in the way. As a woman, she looks farther than a man, I would say. She has good judgment. Many times, after she's been right about something, I realize it later. One example is the house we bought twenty years ago. I was looking to buy in San Clemente, and she gave a lot of reasons not to do it. In the meantime, she looked and looked until one day she found a house in Laguna Niguel. It was kind of beat up, but I fixed it and it turned out to be a good buy. It had a good location and a view. She's very to-the-point. I went with her decision, and it turned out well.

I want to point all this out because people get a false picture of what it is to be a chef. They think you become a movie star. But aside from your personal problems, it's a difficult profession. There's so much to deal with. There's not just the cooking part. There's being a manager and planning dinners. Everybody depends on the chef for so many things. If you have a big group, you want to wow them. You have to figure out a way. A building is a building, whether it's the Ritz-Carlton or the Four Seasons. They're not a meal.

The meal is what it's about. A lunch, dinner, reception, whatever it's going to be, it has to be very well done, so a chef has that pressure to make sure that you don't want to lose a two-million-dollar room. It's a huge judgment on their part. Service is important, but the culinary element is a huge part of a hotel's success. For the chef, the stress level is high. You have employee problems, management problems, so many things.

When you go home, you bring all that with you. You have to keep going and going and going. You don't even have time for friends. It gets lonely on that side of things.

One day after I finished work, I stopped at a bar next door to the restaurant. I knew a lot of French guys went there, so I finally met most of them. They all worked in a nice hotel, called the Stephen F. Austin. I told them my background and what had happened to me. One of the guys named Pascal told me he was the chef at that hotel and was leaving in two months to work at a new hotel in Aspen. It was late May. He was leaving in August to do the opening for the new season. He said "Look, if you want to meet with the general manager for an interview, I know they'll be needing a replacement."

I thought, *Great!* I went to see the general manager who was also French. I did the interview, prepared a tasting, which they liked, and they said, "Okay, you've got a job. You can start in two weeks."

This was my first job as an executive chef in a full-service boutique hotel. My salary went from nine dollars an hour to forty-six thousand a year. This was unbelievable. I was back in the hotel business. Cuca and the kids were happy. This was a company that had bought three hotels and was opening a fourth. They also owned the Sunset Marquis hotel in West Hollywood and the Westwood Marquis, which later became the W Hotels. They bought a very small hotel in Phoenix, Arizona, then they bought the Grand Hotel in Washington, D.C. They also owned movie studios in Hollywood, Raleigh Enterprise. The organization also owned a line of private jets.

The economy in Texas was going south, but the business was still okay. Since the hotel was located close to the State Capitol, every Wednesday we had many politicians come in for lunch. The hotel had two restaurants, one casual and a fine dining place called the Remington Room. I created a lavish seafood buffet every Friday. We were sold out most of the time and turned the Remington Room into a steakhouse, with a few of my special dishes. Brad Johnson, who is now a food critic at the *Orange County Register*, was a server there.

This kept us going until around November of '86. Business really started to hurt throughout that winter; by then we were merely surviving. Since the economy was not doing well, real estate prices were at their lowest.

Toward the end of the summer of 87, I told my wife that we should take advantage of the economy and buy a house. We had enough to make a down payment. But we knew the economy was bad and you could buy houses much cheaper than the market rate. We started to shop around. My budget was no more than ninety-thousand dollars. I could put down up to ten thousand dollars.

The agent took us to one house he knew was for sale. It was listed at one hundred and twenty thousand, way above my budget. It was a modern house, almost three thousand square feet, with four bedrooms. The best of the best you can imagine was in that house. The kitchen was unreal. The backyard was so big, you could play a football game in it. It was a huge, huge lot. The house had a big deck in the back. It was a dream house.

The guy said, "Can you do ninety-five?" That was a lot less than one twenty. He made the offer, and the owner accepted. The guy owned two houses and two businesses. The taxes took him down. He didn't want to lose his main house, so he sold the second one. That's how bad the economy was. That street had twenty-five brand-new houses built, unsold, with nobody living in them, not a soul. People were sneaking into them to steal carpets, cabinets, whatever they could.

The US economy at the time was pretty bad, but it was especially bad in Texas. Many office buildings in downtown Austin were unoccupied.

Texas Instruments was laying off people left and right; Motorola also. I was shocked to see what was going on in the city.

We signed all the papers on the house and opened escrow. One week, ten days, two weeks went by. We were excited. We were going to move into the house in the next ten days. At work, I saw that the numbers were going down in the restaurant. When I started at the restaurant, the average check was thirty to thirty-five dollars. The amounts were going down, so the general manager, in order to generate cash, offered a three-course dinner for fifteen dollars. We were giving it away, basically. We were in survivor mode.

One day in late September 87, we were told that the corporate heads were flying in. The president and vice president, financial officer, and corporate VP of operations were coming for a meal. We needed to meet them for a dinner I prepared. They arrived a couple of hours early and announced to the managers that there would be a general meeting at nine o'clock the next morning for all employees.

I had dinner and went to bed feeling strange. The next morning at nine o'clock, the board of directors arrived in the ballroom for a big meeting for all employees. The company thanked us for all the good work, blah blah blah, but since business had been doing poorly over the last year and year and a half, the decision was to close the next day at five o'clock p.m.

That was a shock. The first thing that came to my mind was, *Oh my God, the house!* I called my realtor and said, "Listen, I have to break the deal. I'm losing my job. I don't know what I'm going to do. I would not be able to pay the mortgage." We had to cancel the deal. I had a letter from my general manager saying we were closing. I showed it to the realtor as proof.

So we stopped everything. Here I was again, going home without a job.

California Dreaming

Where was I going to find a job in Austin? I looked around, checked the newspapers. E-mails didn't exist. I made calls to a few friends. People said they'd get back to me. I sent resumes all over Austin and surrounding areas. I applied to Motorola when I saw in the paper that they were looking for a chef. Two weeks later, I got a phone call. Motorola told me that my Green Card wasn't good anymore.

I said, "What are you talking about? I'm here. I'm legal."

They said, "No, your Green Card is no good."

Two, three weeks went by. There was nothing going on in Austin. I told my wife I would have to look outside. I made calls to friends in California. I didn't have friends anywhere else. A month and a half went by. A friend called. He had worked for Raleigh Enterprise. He said the guy who had been the manager at the Westwood Marquis had bought the Hotel Laguna in Laguna Beach. His name was Claes Anderson. He was Danish and had brought a chef over from Denmark a few months ago who turned out to be terrible. He was looking for a new one. I called Claes, had a quick interview over the phone, and he flew me out to meet in Laguna. After a long interview, he offered me the job, to start mid-November of '87.

I went back home and told my wife, "I have a job. We're going to move to Laguna Beach and the boss will pay, so get ready to pack. In the meantime, I'm going to look for an apartment in Orange County. I'll go by myself and come back to pick you up."

That's what I did. I drove from Austin, Texas, to Laguna Beach, California, in my Oldsmobile and looked for an apartment every day. I found one and flew back home. It was a two-bedroom townhome in Laguna Niguel. The rent was nearly one thousand dollars a month. I drove back from Austin with my wife and kids and started work on December 1st.

My wife wasn't sure about the move. She loved Texas. The people were open and friendly. The lifestyle was good. She loved the atmosphere. But she also loved the apartment in Laguna Niguel. It had a swimming pool and tennis courts. It was a nice complex of forty-eight townhomes, twenty minutes away from work.

Life was good. I worked hard, pulling double shifts every day, to build the quality the hotel needed in order to bring customers in. Anderson was married to an American, with whom he'd managed the Westwood Marquis. He died around 2011. He could drink a bottle of wine a day. By four or five o'clock, he'd be done.

I built the place as if it were my own. I deep cleaned and organized the entire kitchen and designed a light Californian menu with a lot of seafood as we were located on the ocean. The hotel had a fantastic setting, right on the sand next to the main beach. The casual restaurant seated up to 150 people, all outside, with an incredible view. The hotel also had a fine-dining restaurant with a large window on the ocean.

The business took off like a rocket. We went from averaging eighty people a day to 300 within seven months. I made fresh individual pizza with thirty pounds of dough every other day, with all kinds of fresh topping. We were cracking a lot of numbers. In the fine-dining room, we doubled our average count daily. What a difference from Texas that was! We also had one or two weddings a weekend. Live music in the lounge also brought more and more people. It was a great and warm ambiance.

The kitchen was about seventy years old and in bad shape. I worked with whatever I had in building up a reputation in the area. I stayed there two-and-a-half years, but there was never an upgrade. I didn't complain. I did my job. I did the best I could. We went way up. I was proud of that place.

But this was not my niche. I wanted to be back in luxury again.

When I was in Texas, working for the Stephen F. Austin Hotel, the food and beverage director quit. They didn't replace the position because they couldn't. So I took it over to become the chef and the food and beverage director. I was in my office one day reading a magazine article about a famous hotel that had opened in late '85. The name of the hotel was the Ritz-Carlton Laguna Niguel. I read the article, saw the pictures and coverage of the food.

My gosh, how much I would love to be there! How lucky that chef is! I wish to meet him. In Texas, that was a kind of dream. But it was far away.

It motivated me to see a certain kind of food on a plate, with the scenery, a barbecue on the beach, and all kinds of other things connected with a hotel. I said, this was an image I had from when I first wanted to become a chef: the food, the kitchen, the uniform. I wanted to be like that. I did become that, and the image now came back to me.

So one day, at my office in Stephen F. Austin, I called the Ritz-Carlton Hotel and asked to speak to the chef. They put me through. I introduced myself and said I would like to apply for a position as soon as possible. He said they weren't looking right now but would let me know if something opened up.

I never heard any more from him, but the image persisted in my mind. Knowing that I was only three miles away from the Ritz-Carlton, and even though I was working at the Hotel Laguna, one day I drove over and went inside.

I went to the kitchen and met the chef. I told him I was working at the Hotel Laguna and reminded him of the call I had made a year and a half ago. I told him I wished I could work in this hotel. This was my background. I told him that, if he needed help someday doing a special party, I'd come in to help.

We started a relationship based on that visit. A few months later, he called me and said he had a huge event, "The World of Wine," and needed chefs to manpower each buffet station around the main pool.

I went and felt like a little kid again, so impressed by everything, the hotel, the food we were putting together. My gosh, I enjoyed it.

We kept communicating. My wife was taking the kids to school, and in the street near the school, she met a lady one day walking her dog and struck up a conversation. My wife told her that I was French and a chef.

"Oh, my husband is a chef, too," she said, adding, "My husband is a chef at the Ritz-Carlton."

My wife said, "My husband is a chef at the Hotel Laguna."

They started to get friendly. Soon enough, we got an invitation to the house, with the chef, Christian Rassinoux, and his wife and their kids who went to the same school as our kids and became friends on their own.

We all had a lot in common. We became friends. Rassinoux knew that I wanted to work at the Ritz-Carlton. He invited me to a chaine des rotisseurs dinner. It's a membership club you join to pay for up to six special dinner events a year. There can be up to seven courses, including wine pairing. It's a high-end social club where you discover new wine and food.

For me, it was an unbelievable break, because while I was in Texas dreaming about that hotel, I fell two or three years behind in my career. The time went by, and I told Christian that, if he ever had an opening, I would really like to join the staff.

One day we had dinner together and he said his executive sous chef was leaving for Hong Kong to open a new Ritz-Carlton, so if I wanted to take over his position, it wouldn't be like a full chef as I was then, but I'd have a foot in the door.

Of course I said yes. He did the paperwork, I did a couple of interviews, and boom! I had the job.

I gave my notice to the Hotel Laguna. Anderson was not happy to see me go, but said, "That's life." So he wished me the best in my new move. Within a week or two, I interviewed with the Ritz-Carlton's corporate chef who said they were opening two new hotels in the next six months and were looking for a chef. [just one?] He asked me if I'd be interested.

This was unbelievable!

So here I was at the Ritz-Carlton Laguna where I was introduced to a whole new world of cooking and different ethnic foods, Indonesian, Vietnamese, Indian, and more. My kitchen vocabulary expanded tremendously. In fine dining, it was mainly French cuisine. I felt in my element there and enjoyed it. I also had to learn the Ritz discipline, the Ritz vocabulary, and much more. Soon enough, after eight months, I was ready to move on and get ready for the opening of the new Ritz-Carlton Pasadena.

Sierra Madre

 hen the offer was presented to me, I said, "Of course," and thanked God for this beautiful gift he just handed to me. The chef gave me the job to open the Ritz-Carlton in Pasadena, situated in an idyllic spot near the Sierra Madre mountains. This was in late 1990. This opening was projected for the spring of '91. He said, "You will move there early November to be ready to open in March."

A huge task lay ahead of me. I had to build a team consisting of two executive sous chefs, one pastry chef, and twelve sous-chefs. I conducted a lot of interviews and created different concepts for the four restaurants, with different menus. I did a lot of research to look for new ideas and identified all the equipment necessary for every outlet and the main kitchen. It was a new venture and a large undertaking. I started to pray, asking God to send me his wisdom and guide me in this process. I was confident that I could meet the challenge.

The Ritz-Carlton Laguna had set the foundation for me to be successful in the new opening as I had to learn their policies, style of service, and their food and labor costs. There were so many things to learn. I was feeling great. This was the position I always wanted, to be in a luxury hotel, to show what I can do.

November came around, and I went up to Pasadena to prepare for the opening. We had to put a team together for four restaurants. One was for three meals, one was for casual dining with French cuisine, one was a steakhouse, and the last was the pool and lobby lounge. Of course, banquets were a huge part of the business. For those, I had to search for a Michelin-rated chef from France. This was the norm for the Ritz, and it was not easy to achieve. He had to have a minimum of one star in the Michelin guide. But then, none of the ones we contacted spoke English. This was very challenging

In the meantime, I had to do all my work for the opening: interviews, menu, tasting, the banquet menu, china, and so on. Without exaggeration, I worked sixteen hours a day. I started in the morning between 6:30 and 7 o'clock and stayed until 9:30 or 10 at night. This was the first opening I had ever done. I was still living in Laguna and had to drive back and forth. It was seventy-two miles one way. I did that for two months and told my wife it was becoming too difficult, so we rented a house in La Canada-Flintridge, near Pasadena, to be closer to work. It was only fifteen minutes away, which was a big help for me. But it was still a big sacrifice because I couldn't see the kids. I worked six days a week to get ready for the opening. We had to enroll them in new schools, which was difficult for them to adapt to again. They already had a problem with the languages. They had forgotten their French in the years we spent in Mexico, and I didn't speak it at home. I had so little time with them. Then when we moved to Texas, they had to learn and speak English. It had been tough on them.

The good thing was that my wife continued to speak Spanish, so they never completely lost it. It was good to be bilingual.

A lot of people from Pasadena were anticipating the hotel's new opening and were very excited. It had been closed for four years, became a Sheraton, and was condemned after the big earthquake. There were huge cracks in the foundation that forced it to close down. Then a real estate company from Florida took over. They put a lot of money into it, $150 million. The Ritz-Carlton was hired to manage the hotel, the twentieth to open in the chain.

At the time, 1991, real estate was not doing well. The Florida company was losing money. We fell two months behind in the completion of the hotel.

The opening was postponed twice. The hotel ballrooms and banquet rooms were completely booked every day starting at the end of March. Special parties, weddings, groups, you name it. Every day. Since we had postponed the opening, that cost a lot of money, too. We put back the opening until early April, then again at the end of April.

Finally, we said we had to open even though we were not ready. We were still missing ten per cent of the staff. The refrigeration was not completed. Cable was missing. The dishwasher had not been installed. Stuff like that.

So we opened at less than one hundred per cent ready, without refrigeration. Pasadena is an old city. People had been waiting for the hotel to open for years. They were making a lot of plans. The hotel was situated in a wealthy area, near San Marino. They wanted to party. Anticipation was high.

I proceeded with my presentation to all Ritz-Carlton corporate employees. Every dish was presented and described for every restaurant. We opened, but the result was not great. People on staff began to quit. They couldn't work under the conditions. There was a lot of pressure.

One week after the opening, the real estate company that owned the hotel declared bankruptcy. They had no more cash. That meant no more revenue flow into the hotel. We couldn't pay the bills. Everything had to be COD. Every time I called my vendors for products to be delivered, they asked me for a check or there would be no delivery.

It became very difficult to operate in those conditions. I could not plan ahead, specifically for banquets. I couldn't place orders. People were quitting. I didn't have the product to do the work. There was still no refrigeration. We were missing working tables. People were screaming left and right. There was a lot of pressure on me. I pushed as much as I could, working eighteen hours a day.

Then of course there were more problems at home because I was there less and less. My wife wondered what was going on. "I don't see you anymore." My general manager blamed everybody else for everything that went wrong.

The first thing he did when he saw me at seven o'clock in the morning was blame me for what went bad the day before. But the problems were out of my hands, and instead of finding a solution, he was adding more problems to the existing ones.

I kept doing as much as I could, to the point where I said, "I can't do this anymore. I don't think it's worth it." I told my wife, "That's it."

I'd given a hundred and fifty per cent to the hotel for nine nine months. It became a mess. They're borrowing money to put into it. We lost two major managers. One couldn't handle the volume of complaints. The other was the financial director. He could not deal with the owners and Ritz corporation.

Finally I couldn't take it anymore. I meditated and asked God for guidance. I was not feeling good at all—me, who wanted so badly to work in a luxury hotel. I was on the edge.

But the answer was clear: to put my family first and take care of them.

I gave the general manager notice that I was leaving in two weeks. It was difficult for me to make that decision because I'm not a person who gives up. But coming in every day was utterly depleting.

Luckily enough, a few days before I made that decision, I talked to Christian Rassinoux. He'd been working for the Ritz-Carlton for about seven years. I told him I couldn't do it anymore. I couldn't sleep from the stress.

He understood and said that an upscale country club in Coto de Caza, in south Orange County, was opening. It was owned by Chevron, the gas and oil company. They wanted employees from the Ritz-Carlton to staff it.

This was fantastic for me. Within two weeks of quitting the Ritz-Carlton, I had a new job. So we moved back South and changed schools once again for the kids. We had to look for a new house. I told the kids I was sorry we had to put them through another change, but that this would be the last time.

Country Club Life

S o I started at the Coto de Caza Golf and Racquet Club in the fall of 1991. It used to be an old ranch-style club with horses and stables. There had been maybe eighty horses up there. Chevron bought the entire Coto de Caza property and developed a golf course. They built a new clubhouse restaurant that needed staffing. I was the chef. The food and beverage director came from the Ritz-Carlton in St. Louis. With him and a few others from the Ritz-Carlton chain, we made a good team.

We opened two restaurants, one casual, the other designed for fine dining. We were only open four days a week, Thursday through Sunday. We did weddings. We developed a good customer base. The club had three hundred and fifty to four hundred members. We created a lot of fun things for the membership. I became Chef Freddy for all members. They loved it.

I developed a cooking class that met once a week with twenty members. We did two hours of cooking. I enjoyed it. We did all the basic kinds of cooking, from braising to roasting, to stock, like chicken and fish. At the end of six months, we created a buffet prepared by the students for all the members. About three hundred people came, and after the dinner, we staged an award ceremony. We did this every year. [for how long?]

I also created a menu for food to go, for members only: good dishes like grilled salmon, beef filet mignon, Asian chicken, and some Italian entrees as well. People didn't always have the opportunity to cook at home, and since we were open only four days a week, sometimes they ordered stuff already prepared, to eat at home, or customized by me, whatever they wanted. They were very happy. We did a lot of golf tournaments with special buffets created by chefs we brought in from all over Orange County. It was fun.

I was there for three years, from late '91 to December of '94. Then I got the news that Chevron had sold the clubhouse to Club Corp of America. It's a group that runs maybe fifty or sixty clubs throughout the United States. One day the corporation representatives came into the clubhouse and said they'd be the new operators. I interviewed them. They said unfortunately they would not be able to hire me under their new management, because they were not going to do upscale cuisine. They were going to do basic clubhouse stuff: burgers, sandwiches, a couple of salads, that's it.

"So we don't need a chef like you. Thank you very much."

That was November. They were taking over January 1st. They gave me thirty days and no severance package.

I told my wife that I would look in the area for another job. I was a little dispirited because this was happening again, and again I was faced with the question about what I was going to do next. I thought about my kids. They were going to a beautiful Catholic high school that had opened in Coto de Caza just a couple of years earlier, called Santa Margarita High.

They had a highly ranked athletic program. Every Friday I would prepare pre-game meals for the varsity football team at Saddleback College stadium. At six o'clock, the bus would drive the team to the Saddleback college stadium to get ready for the seven-fifteen kickoff. At five o'clock, I made them a steak dinner. When I cut New York steaks at the clubhouse, I'd always end up with end cuts I couldn't sell. So I gave them to the school. At the end of the week, I'd collect a minimum of twenty-five steaks. It was just enough for the team. I'd cook baked potatoes, steak, vegetables, and dessert for the team. At five o'clock, we all sat down, the players and coaches, for dinner. At quarter to six, they'd get on the bus and go. So they had a good meal before the game.

One of the players I fed over two seasons was Carson Palmer. He went on to be a Heisman Award winner at USC and was drafted by the Cincinnati Bengals. My son was on the Margarita football team as well. He played running back. He wanted to play quarterback, but he wasn't tall enough. He was only five nine. He couldn't look over his linemen to see the defense, so he only made the B team and was a backup runner on the varsity.

I enjoyed the three-and-a-half years I was there. I enjoyed the school and the church where we did quite a few catering affairs. I really was involved in many of the activities in the area. Unfortunately, when the club got sold, I had to get ready to move on again.

December went by. I put my resume out with about six or seven headhunters, plus sending out a few myself. For the whole month I received only a couple of phone calls. It was a desperate time. Six weeks went by. I still had to pay the bills, including high school, which now included my younger son.

At that time, the school was charging six hundred a month for each kid, plus all the expenses for their sports equipment. I had to make my house and car payments. I was literally living on credit cards. I had three cards that I used to the max. I paid the minimum each month. I couldn't get out of debt. It was lucky that, when I moved to the Ritz-Carlton and had that La Canada place, I was able to save a little money. I had been making a good salary. So with that little bit of money, I had just barely enough to put the down payment on the house, which had been in foreclosure. It was lucky for me. The payments on the house were fourteen hundred dollars a month. School was twelve hundred dollars a month for both my sons. There were the car and insurance payments; the list went on and on and on. I needed five thousand dollars a month. I wasn't making it. I couldn't save a penny.

The good thing was that, while I was at the club, I had a lot more free time with my wife and kids, which I enjoyed. And I worked on the house, fixing the backyard, changing this, doing that, which, in the long run, paid off.

In the meantime, I was looking for a job. We are now early in '95. I had to move out at the end of November. All this time, December through January, there was nothing. I was desperate.

All of a sudden, I got a call out of the blue, in late January. It was from the Westin South Coast Plaza. They said they got my resume through a headhunter and would like to talk to me. Can I come for an interview?

I did. They said, "This hotel has high marks. We've been open since '81. All the way through '92 we've done splendid business serving prominent social people in the area, who have come for a lot of different functions.

"We had a chef who ruined everything. Over the past two years, we've lost sixty per cent of our business."

According to them, the chef was arrogant, inexperienced, lazy, and worked only six hours a day in the kitchen, coming in at nine o'clock and leaving at three and not taking care of anything. The quality had gone down the drain. People complained. Finally, the Westin management had to fire him.

Now they were looking for a chef who could help them regain what they'd lost over the past two years. They asked if I thought I could do that. I said, "Sure. Why not? This has been my life for the past thirty years. Yes, I can do it."

I did a tasting for them. They liked it and offered me the job. This was February of '95. My mission was to bring back those old diners. Since it's only eighteen miles to Coto de Caza, we didn't have to move again.

Fifi Chao was the food critic for the *Business Journal* in Orange County. Everyone knew her. She created a club for dining out. She came to check on the food in the first month I was there. I wanted to put something special on the menu, something different and a bit exotic, consisting of items we did not find anywhere. So I made a sweetbread, pork cheeks, veal kidney, rabbit—dishes you had to work harder to make, but unique. We were excited to have her. A lot of people followed her recommendations.

I was proud of my new menu. She tried three or four different things. I went out to see her. We only spoke briefly.

A week or ten days later, the review came out. Oh my God, she cut me down. I don't remember what she wrote, but the article was very damaging.

The general manager was not happy. He told me to change the menu right away and do something more approachable for everybody.

We waited a few months. We apologized to Fifi Chao and invited her back. She accepted. It was wow! She raved about the menu, the food, the new creations, and the flair from my own Provence. She put me at the top of the list. We became good friends. We'd call each other once in a while.

Once again, the restaurant was okay. We were doing all right. But the banquets were a big job. With the team I had, it was very difficult. They weren't working well. They stole food. Security wouldn't believe it and said to me, "We've been here for twenty years. No one has ever stolen anything from here."

I said, "Are you sure of that?"

There were three coolers to the left of my office door. From a corner, you could see all three. I knew stuff was disappearing from my coolers. So one day I set a trap. I put five pounds of shrimp on the shelf inside the walk-in cooler. I would see tomorrow if the shrimps were still there, because it was not a product we used often in the restaurant; nobody needed them during the night.

The next morning, we went to clean out the cooler—No shrimps. I went to the security office. I said I wanted to see the tape from last night. We ran it back. One o'clock, two o'clock in the morning, ah, we see a guy approaching the cooler with a large trash can on wheels. What's that guy doing? He went inside the cooler with the trash can for three or four minutes before he came out again. Then he took the same can out to the dock. I couldn't prove the shrimp were in it, but when I came in at seven in the morning and nobody had ordered shrimp during the night but it was gone, clearly that guy had been stealing.

They called a detective and conducted an interview with the guy. He admitted that he was taking stuff out almost every day, beef, shrimp—you name it. He'd been stealing for years.

There were other bad apples: cooks who didn't follow instructions, cooks who were arrogant or wouldn't accept my changes in the kitchen. They didn't want to improve the quality of the food, the recipes, and so many other things. They were against any of my improvements.

So I fired one of them. The HR director came into the kitchen the next day. She was furious and said, "You cannot fire people just like that."

I replied, "I have a mission here to bring clientele back. I can't do it with those cooks. They are impossible."

A week later, I fired another guy. The HR director was mad about that too. One morning—I had three cooks left—one didn't show up. The next day we were busy with a banquet, and they knew it. Not one cook showed up in the kitchen. They all called in sick. It was just to show me who was the boss. I said to myself, "They want to play a game with me, but we'll see who wins." I quickly prayed to God for his guidance and support and not to abandon me in these difficult situations.

Then I went to the dishwashers and said, "Come with me." I spoke Spanish. I told them, "I need your help. You just have to follow my instructions and not worry. Everything will be fine."

We served every banquet, on time. I was sweating bullets, but we made it.

The next day the cooks all came back to work, and since they already had quite a few write-ups on file, I said, "Know what? You don't have a job here. Out of my kitchen."

The next day, they came back to work, and I told them they could either follow me or go back to where they'd been. One quit, and one stayed and became a good cook, actually. He had an influence on the others. He'd been hard-headed, but he changed. I told them that the only way we could do good work and presentations was not to cut corners, to put your love into your work, and give it one hundred percent.

We built up a new team in the kitchen. We changed the menus. I created more business. I picked up a group of dentists who came once a month as a club and spent a lot of money because I made them five and six course dinners. We got good articles, and we began booking a lot of returning parties. Word spread pretty quickly in Orange County society about the Westin South Coast Plaza. We received a lot of award nominations and won a silver plate, sponsored by an organization like Zagat. We retrieved everything we had lost. People were happy to come back.

From Coast to Desert

*O*n mid-'96, Starwood Hotels bought the Westin company. They also bought the Sheraton. A month after Starwood took over, the CEO came to meet all of us at the hotel, and of course many changes came with it. A couple of them had a big impact in my department. The first was to close the fine-dining room; the other one was to close my pastry shop. All those changes were to go into effect in a few days. How was I going to do my pastry now? I had to lay off five pastry cooks and a pastry chef. That was not a pretty sight. They were upset. People had been working there for eight to ten years. I had to call other friends at other hotels to see if they were looking for cooks. I found one or two but not enough for everybody.

I had to find a place that could supply me with desserts and duplicate the desserts I had in my banquet menu. We were hosting a lot of banquets. Luckily enough, I found a pastry shop run by an old friend. I gave him my recipes, and he said, "I will make them for you." That was nice.

Basically, I had no gaps between what we made and what was provided for us. Of course it cost us much more money and the food cost went up, but then I saved on labor.

So we kept on as usual. Then Starwood started to look for someone to take over the restaurant. Quite a few candidates came, like Michel Richard and Wolfgang Puck. There was not too much interest until Joaquim Spichel came. He owned more than 40 restaurants but was famous for starting Patina Restaurant Group and was looking to develop a restaurant along the lines of Pinot. He had Pinot Gris, Pinot Blanc, Pinot Noir. He had four or five already established.

When the Starwood CEO visited on a weekend, we had a long meeting. They were very finance oriented and had already sealed the book on their hotels and the restaurants, which were losing money.

After he announced that they planned to close the restaurant, we asked, "How are we going to provide room service to people who are staying at the hotel?" They said they would find an operator from outside who would take over the restaurant.

Spichel looked at the place and was interested. He was thinking of opening a restaurant called Pinot Provence, which he did. My role was just to help them. We shared a little bit of the kitchen and the stove until they built their own kitchen. The restaurant was transformed into a very nice dining facility called Pinot Provence. I helped them open the space. They brought the entire decor from Provence. It was beautiful and reminded me of my youth. The chef who opened the space was Florent Marmeau. I gave him a hand in the beginning, as I was still on the Westin payroll. But Pinot Provence was a completely independent operation that paid rent against a percentage of the gross.

As time went by, my interest began declining. I had only banquets. Because the menu was pretty set, there wasn't much more for me to do. My creativity was not challenged. The work became monotonous. A year went by, during which I questioned myself, "What am I doing here?" I was getting bored and knew I needed to look for something else to do.

I was still living in Coto de Caza. One of my sons graduated from high school in '96. The other was ready to graduate in '99. I had offers from Westin to go to Manila, Shanghai, and Germany. I talked them over with my wife. She said forget about Manila. She didn't really care about Asia in general, and Germany was too cold, damp, and far from California. And just to think moving the kids again was not in her best interest.

So I looked around locally. It took me a while until finally I had an offer from a very-high-end private club in Palm Desert, called Bighorn Golf Club. It was prestigious; it had a clubhouse, seven or eight hundred members, and an annual membership fee of $18,000 and an initial fee of $250,000.

The owner, a philanthropist, R. D. Hubbard, was selling lots ready for building houses whose selling price was a million and a half—just the lots. To build a house on one would cost three or four million dollars.

I got the job, and my goodness, the owners and operators knew nothing—and I mean nothing—about food and beverage operations. They were one hundred per cent into the golf business. They only wanted to impress people about food and beverages simply because people were paying a lot of money. They wanted to have a beautiful club, a beautiful dining room, and good food. But they didn't know how to make it work.

As soon as I started the new job, I saw many things that were not in line with the requirements of a luxury club, such as china and glassware for the restaurant. So I suggested to the owner the need to invest in a complete new tableware set (china, silver, glasses) and better kitchen equipment. In a meeting with the boss and the GM, they totally disapproved of the expenses. They thought it unnecessary to have nice china and glassware in order to serve good food in a fine-dining restaurant. They also disagreed about the need for better kitchen equipment; they thought it was not enough justification for the expense. Yet they were spending millions on the gold course.

This irritated me because it looked like they didn't want me to succeed. Still, I created a beautiful menu for the restaurant. People were happy, but I didn't have support from the management. It was difficult to operate in an atmosphere like that, with no support and no one else with a passion for the effort.

Within a few months, there was a big influx of people buying lots and building houses on them. The clubhouse was getting busier, more large tournaments were taking place, and many more events were scheduled at the club. The demand for in-house private catering grew tremendously.

Now the boss came to me with the idea of developing a catering business in addition to cooking at the club. This was a great opportunity to get new equipment in the kitchen. I created an entirely different menu adapted for catering. The area was isolated. The people who owned those homes were proud of them and liked to serve parties of up to a hundred. I was becoming happy and excited about all those new ventures.

Something I didn't consider was the transport of the food. The club had an open pickup truck, but it wasn't big enough, and to load it with heavy rocks of food would be a dangerous task. I needed a bigger truck with a lift gate. I went to the boss again to ask for a truck with a liftgate, and guess what? He refused and became annoyed by my suggestion.

All my excitement about all those new ideas went down the drain. The more I pleaded for help, the less I got. This was ridiculous. I was even more disappointed when I knew how much money the boss spent on golf course equipment and replacing all the greens for no necessary reason.

This was baffling, but I had to stay focused on what I was there to do. It was even more disturbing when I entered one of those 6,000-thousand-square-feet humongous houses. Their kitchens were a dream. In the garages were Rolls-Royces, Ferraris, Maseratis, all barely driven. The people who owned those houses lived in them for only three or four months of the year. Otherwise they lived in New York or Chicago or Europe. They didn't even take their cars with them. To see all this did nothing to lift my spirit.

Mr. Hubert owned one of those houses. He owned a painting that was worth seven million dollars. It was large and wide, probably twenty feet long, and showed Indians and cowboys. He had a sculpture in bronze of a horse in his entryway that was the size of an actual horse. He had another property in New Mexico and flew from there to Palm Springs and back in a private jet. When he arrived at the Palm Springs airport, he'd take a private helicopter to a green on the golf course, and a chauffeur would pick him up in his Rolls-Royce and drive him the quarter mile to his house.

Hubert was a multimillionaire who invested in real estate again and again and built an empire.

I catered a party at his house for his birthday in late 2000. All the setups were outside, and some of the best golfers in the world were among the 150 guests, including Tiger Woods and Sergio Garcia. I created an international theme with action food stations from different countries. We served whole Maine lobster, grilled sea scallops seared on the plancha, whole lamb being roasted on a pit Mediterranean style, sashimi and sushi made at the station, Korean BBQ and Vietnamese soup station, and much more. Dessert was presented as a big chocolate show with fondue, bomboms, cake and cremeux, a sculpture, and more. At the bar was the entire collection of Opus 1, starting from 1979, brought up from the boss's wine cellar. It was a memorable event.

But this didn't change his decision not to buy me the truck. I kept going, however, and did the best I could. The only reward I had was the knowledge that all the members were very happy. But the lack of support and appreciation from the owner and management was affecting my self-esteem more and more.

I told my wife that I was not happy there. She said, "What do you want to do?"

Chicago: Hotel Sofitel

*T*hen September 11, 2001, happened.

We'd been on a three-month vacation from July to September; it was very hot in Palm Spring during the summer and all the members were gone anyway. The club management called me on September 12th to tell me they might not need a chef for a while. I was not too happy anyway, so I said okay.

I started to look around again for another job, knocking on doors. I looked around Laguna Niguel and Dana Point. I skipped Palm Springs. Nothing was going on there. I saw in the newspaper that the St. Regis had opened in Dana Point, summer 2001. After I was let go from the club in September, I went to see the St. Regis, but of course they were laying off people because there was no business. I talked to the chef, and he said that, if and when they were hiring again, he would call me back; "keep in touch."

I kept looking. Two weeks later, at the end of September, he called to say that business was picking up quickly. He'd laid off quite a few people and now needed to rehire. He didn't have a good position for me because he'd kept all his sous-chefs, but he asked if I'd like to work for him anyway and I said of course. So I went there in early October and helped him. At least it was something with which to provide for my family. I stayed until December helping with banquets, doing different things, helping him train and put his team back together, even though I knew I couldn't stay there.

In December, he said it was up to me if I wanted to stay on as a lead cook; that was the only position he had to offer. At the same time, business was coming back vigorously. The Ritz-Carlton Laguna across the street was desperate for help. So I went with them.

Here I was in early January, back at the Ritz-Carlton, with better wages. It was still like a dream but real. I helped Christian, the chef, with all his needs, from garde manger to banquets and fine dining. In the meantime, I was still looking and prayed for a better job. I could not stay doing this forever.

In early February, I got a call from a good friend, Kurt Fischer. He was the corporate food and beverage director when I was with Westin and now was consulting for Sofitel, a French hotel. He had great news: the Sofitel Chicago was scheduled to open in June, and they were looking for a chef.

Right away I discussed it with my wife. Chicago is not Miami when it comes to weather. She had a bad image of Chicago. It had a lot of crime. It was cold. I said, "It's a great opportunity. I can establish my name there." Besides, there was nothing else available, and I needed a job badly. She finally agreed and said, "Go ahead. I hope you will be successful."

I called Kurt. I was excited once again. My prayers had been answered, thanks be to God.

I went to do a tasting at the Sofitel in New York, actually, on February 14, 2002. They were blown away, as I was the fifth chef to do a tasting and interview. I made crisp Maine lobster spring rolls, Asian petite greens, double lamb chops stuffed with sweet breads wrapped in spinach and caul fat with porcini polenta, a basil crème brulee, pistachio ice cream and tuile for dessert. They wanted mid-Italian, Provencal cuisine and something Asian.

I had learned my lesson from earlier tastings serving as advice: don't do anything too difficult, because you only have one chance. Different kitchens have different equipment. Sometimes you have no help. The odds have to be beatable. It is not easy on your mind if you're worrying whether you'll get this job or not. You've got to keep it simple, creative, seasonal as much as possible, and made in a clean, colorful presentation. Of course, it has to taste great.

The protein needs to be cooked perfectly. Timing is also an issue. And keep the kitchen clean and organized.

When I walked into the kitchen the day of the tasting, I was confident. I focused 100 % on every detail. I described every dish to the general manager, corporate food and beverage, and director of operations.

Within 10 minutes after the tasting, they called me in the dining room, and after a quick interview, they made me an offer. I could not believe how fast it went, so fast that I asked them for a couple of days to talk it over with my wife.

I immediately called her to relay the news. On the flight back, my mind was going 100 miles an hour. I really needed to resharpen my knife. Everything I did at the Ritz Pasadena was coming back; the only difference was that it was now ten years later. I needed to update my cooking style, ideas, and technique if I wanted to be competitive with the Peninsula, Four

Seasons, Park Hyatt, and Ritz-Carlto—hotels that were just within a block from the Sofitel, incidentally.

Two days later, the actual offer arrived by FedEx. I accepted and moved to Chicago in late February.

It was still winter and very cold. It isn't called the windy city for nothing. I got sick a week after I arrived. I thought I would die. It was some kind of flu. I had a fever. I didn't know what to do. Construction of the Sofitel wasn't finished yet, so they put me in a hotel next door where I worked out of a small office.

By contract, I had a month to find my own apartment. I didn't have a car. I was on a budget because I still had to pay my mortgage in California. So I couldn't afford to pay for a taxi every time I went out to look for an apartment to live in. I had to take the bus and walk up to four or five blocks to look for a place. The wind was terrible. I remember one night when I called my wife and I couldn't hear her because of the noise from the wind.

I found a place about fifteen miles from the hotel after I'd looked at three or four others. They were terrible. They were either dirty and old, or they were very expensive. They had noisy elevators. With only one week left, I didn't know what to do. Finally, a lady from the hotel where I was staying asked if I was still looking. When she found out how far from work I was traveling, she recommended a place that was only four blocks from the hotel.

I went to look at the apartment building, which was next to the Hancock Building. It was built around 1928. She showed me one apartment, a very old studio. The window was as thin as a piece of paper. When you put your hand near it, you felt the cold from outside. The door to the bathroom didn't close. The entire bathroom was no more than fifteen square feet. The sink was no more than a foot wide. If you stood up from the toilet, you banged into the sink, which kept the door from opening completely. Two people couldn't fit into the bathroom. And the apartment was already a thousand dollars a month. This was in 2002.

I rented it. I had to buy a bed and a couple of chairs and pots and pans. Every week I had to buy something. Anyway, I was so tied up at the hotel, working eighteen hours a day, seven days a week, in preparation for the opening at the end of May, and living alone, that I did really care about the furniture of the studio.

Here I was again, starting from nothing, looking for the best players for my culinary team, in a city where I didn't know anyone. I questioned myself a few times: "How will I succeed?" I put all my worries in the hands of God and asked him for support. My wife was in California. I felt lonely in front of the big task. But the next day I felt great.

I enjoyed creating my cuisine. I found a good executive sous-chef who helped me a lot. The restaurant, called Cafe des Architectes, had a Mediterranean theme. Banquets were more varied, serving Asian, Middle Eastern, and American food. The design of the hotel was very modern. The architect [name?] received the award for the best design worldwide for 2002. When I saw the vessels, they were the best of the best, all new collections from Villeroy and Boch. The buffet tables were very slick, with brushed nickel on top—no need for a tablecloth. It looked very chic and gave me more ideas for creating dishes. I met a lot of people in those first months. Chicago was very welcoming, with a lot of great chefs who formed a great community.

We had to prepare something spectacular for the grand opening and the dignitaries in attendance: the mayor of Chicago, the French minister of agriculture, the governor of Illinois, and other French politicians as well.

We did a fabulous opening. Great articles came out. We took a lot of business from the Four Seasons and the Park Hyatt. The hard work and many hours had paid off. The Sofitel became the number one destination for Sunday brunch in Chicago. Reservations were taken for weeks ahead. People stood in the cold for half an hour waiting to get in. We created a typical French petit dejeuner, with a basket of mini individual baguette, croissant, chocolatine, and almond danish—all freshly baked in the morning—and the cafe presse on each table. The fruit jam was home made as well. What a success!

My wife came for the first time at the end of May when the weather was better. She spent all summer with me in that terrible apartment. She joined a painting school, two of them actually. One was called the Palette and Chisel, which was famous for enrolling a lot of women artists in its workshop. The other was the school from the Chicago Museum of Art. She had started her interest in art about a year before that and met a lot of artists in Chicago. The students at both places were really good, so she was able to get involved in a lot of great stuff. She has so much talent that she mastered her classes very quickly.

Then by the end of September, she left and came back to Southern California. By that time my boys were old enough to take care of themselves. My younger son was twenty-two and working while going to college. My other son was in France, studying foreign business. He was twenty-five.

We were pretty successful in Chicago, taking business from the surrounding hotels. The Sofitel look and ambiance were very hip. The bar was the highlight of the city. News articles named us the best bar of the city and the best breakfast a la Francaise.

Within a year after the restaurant opened, I was approached by a producer from PBS. They were doing a one-hour weekly food show, a food show, aired nationally. There was one chef from Miami, New York, Chicago, San Francisco, Los Angeles, Seattle, New Orleans, Boston, and Dallas, nine in all. It was named At the Chef's Table. It was about a guy who loved cooking and needed a chef to help him to cook a dinner that would impress his special guests.

In my episode, I had to create a five-course menu. The show was divided into four segments of fifteen minutes. The beginning consisted of meeting the host and explaining why he needed a chef like me. Then I had to go to the market with him to look for the best French cheeses (of course we had to smell all of them before we chose the one we liked). Then I took him to a unique place for duck and foie gras. I didn't want him to know where we were going, so I blindfolded him before I took him there. This was the producer's idea. When we got there, I took the blindfold off, and he said, "Wow, I've never seen so many ducks and foie gras in my entire life." He was very pleasantly surprised.

I was happy in Chicago. It was the best city to finally express what I liked to make best: sweet bread, pork feet, venison, foie gras, and much more, products that I never could do anywhere else. People there really enjoyed it. They go all out for dinner and to enjoy food. The quality of the meat was unbelievable, the best I've ever had. We got the best fish from Europe, Australia, and South America. It was incredible to see how fresh they were. When I put sturgeon on the menu, everyone was shocked how good it was. For me it was like a dream. I felt like I was back in the future.

Beside my daily duties running the kitchen, I was involved in many charities. This was very rewarding to me, to be able to give back to society and those most in need and for medical research. The city was beautiful eight months of the year. People enjoyed the outdoors and having lunch and dinner on the terrace. But winter was brutally cold, and it was difficult at times to be separated from my wife for a long period of time, though I had to make the sacrifice. Cuca came to live with me only in the summers, painting in different places. As soon as the weather began getting cold, she'd move back to California. I'd fly back three or four times a year to spend a long weekend with her.

I enjoyed Chicago, but my wife was in Orange County. The separation was more and more difficult. I patiently remained in Chicago trusting God that he would give me an opportunity closer to home. I sent my resume to a couple of hotels, without luck. One was the Four Seasons in Aviara, in Carlsbad. The chef was leaving to start his own restaurant. I applied, but they already had a replacement

So I patiently remained in Chicago praying and trusting God that he will give me an opportunity closer to home. I kept waiting and praying.

I kept a good relationship with the chef of the St. Regis Monarch Beach resort, the one I helped in 2001. One day, he called and said that, if I wanted to be sous-chef, a position was available. I said that was nice, but the pay would be so low that I wouldn't be able to afford it. So I passed.

I kept working until one day, in February of 2006, I was attending the annual chefs' convention of all Sofitels, in Las Vegas. I got a phone call the first day I arrived. It was from Azmin, the chef at the St. Regis. He said he was leaving to open his own restaurant. Six chefs were already interviewing and doing tastings, so he wanted to give me the opportunity to try. Was I interested? Of course I was.

He emailed me the list of things I needed to do for the tasting. It was three pages long. Oh, my God.

I called him back and asked, "Why so much? Was it necessary to do all these things?"

He said, "Do you want to do it or not?"

"Of course I do."

"Then do it."

I started to work on the list. He said I needed to be there in two days because he had to wrap things up quickly. I was one of the last to be interviewed, and they wanted to give me a chance. I said, "Okay," but I was in the middle of a convention. That night, all the chefs were going out for dinner. After a five o'clock meeting, everyone got dressed and ready to go out. "Come on," they said. I told them I was tired and wasn't feeling good. I didn't want to tell them I was putting together a tasting.

I went to my room and worked until two o'clock in the morning. Then I emailed my market list. I waited for a couple of days, finished the convention, and flew back to Chicago. I booked a flight for the next day and told my GM that I had to go back to California; something had happened at home. I took my stuff and flew back for a three-day stay. I had a day and a half of preparation.

The day I arrived, I didn't stop until late at night. The next day I worked eighteen hours. There were things on the requirement list that I'd never done before, like a complete authentic Japanese breakfast. Why a Japanese breakfast for a tasting? I researched it myself and called a Japanese chef to ask how to do it. It was a new experience, and I didn't have time to practice before.

On the third day, the tasting was scheduled for ten o'clock in the morning. It had to be finished by twelve, and I had to present a lot: for the banquet, a plated lunch and dinner, a buffet reception, 3 courses for one bistro, four courses for a gourmet restaurant including some amuse bouche, and a couple of dishes for the pool. It was a lot.

My flight back to Chicago was booked for that afternoon at 2:30 p.m., so I had to leave the hotel by 1:00 p.m. At ten o'clock sharp, I started the tasting, one dish after the other, non-stop. I was sweating big drops. Eight people were there to taste and comment on the food. Thank God, everything went okay. I cleaned up the kitchen quickly, then was ready to go. The chef said, "Thank you. We'll let you know."

I left, went back to Chicago to work in my regular routine.

The days went by. A week went by, two weeks, almost three weeks. No phone call. I lost a bit of my hope. When you do a tasting, they let you know within a week. But deep inside me, I never completely lost hope. I think my faith kept me going and didn't want to let go.

I called the chef and asked if it was any decision done yet. "Am I out?"

"No, no, no, you're still in the race, but we have some debating to do. Sorry for the delay. I think they want to see you back again. The owners want to have an interview with you."

I said okay. A couple of days later, I had to fly back to see the owner and the general manager of the hotel. They picked me up at the airport in a limo. I did an interview with the owner at his house. I answered some questions, then went back to the hotel to speak with the GM and the food and beverage director.

The next day, my flight was again at 2:30 p.m. I was in the main dining room with the controller, having an early lunch, when the director of HR came to see me and said, "Are you leaving today?"

I said, "Yes, I'm leaving in forty-five minutes."

"Oh my goodness. Wait for me."

He went back to his office with the GM. I waited until it was getting on to one o'clock, then I saw the HR guy appear with the GM, carrying a big envelope. They said, "We'd like to make you an offer. Take this with you when you go. We don't need an answer right now, but please let us know as soon as possible if you're okay with this."

It was a big surprise to me. I took the envelope and left. I read it on the plane. The offer was pretty good. It meant I'd be able to come home. I called my wife who was visiting her sister in Mexico. I said, "Guess what? I got a job offer at the St. Regis Monarch Beach resort." She was happy, too. It was great news. All the hard work in the tasting and presentation had paid off. I gave my notice to my general manager in Chicago, and a month later, I was on my way back to California. They gave me a big party. They didn't want to see me go. It was a little sad.

I developed some amazing and memorable dishes during this time: a duck breast with caramelized quince and foie gras and wrapped in slightly smoked bacon. I added a sauce made of calvados, an apple alcohol. I won second place in a Taste of Elegance contest in Illinois in 2004. Another was a pork tenderloin marinated with smoked chili. I lightly smoked the tenderloin too, in cherry wood. That was in Chicago in 2003 Then I did a braised red cabbage served hollowed out in yellow beets. Then I created a sturgeon with sea urchins, champagne, and spuma blended into a foam.

While I was in Chicago, many good things happened to me. First, in 2004, I had the honor and privilege to be elected Maître Cuisinier de France, which was a huge award for me. I received it in Portland, Oregon. Every year the ceremony is held in a different city. I also became the Bailli conseiller Culinaire de Chicago for La Chaine des Rotisseurs. Every month I had to organize a reception and a seven-course dinner in different hotels of the city. After the menu was created by the chef of each hotel, I conducted a tasting with the wine pairing to make sure that every course was up to the standard of the organization. Same thing with each wine, to see if the pairing was done correctly with the food. That was the time to fix details on each dish and the presentation, portion size, and taste. The high-end dinner consisted of up to seven courses, and before the dinner, there was a champagne reception with some canapes. This was another learning experience, working closely with many other chefs.

The guests paid about two hundred and fifty dollars each for dinner. There were 80 members in the society of La Chaine, and we did those dinners once a month. This kept me very busy among so many other things, but I enjoyed every moment of it.

Then we moved on to the produce market and the fish market. At the fish market, we bought a few whole French rouget that weighed about 6 oz. each with the head on. So we got everything we needed and came back to the hotel. The next segment was about the preparation in the kitchen. This took place in the open kitchen of the fine dining at the hotel. There we started to make the mise en place, first showing the host how to devein the foie gras without breaking it, then the cleaning and cutting of all vegetables, followed by the deboning of a duck breast and how to make the marination for it. The most funny part was when I taught him how to filet the French Rouget. He tried to do one and destroyed it, so for the purpose of the show, I screamed and got upset, trying to duplicate Chef Gordon Ramsey The next and last segment of the show focus on the people arriving, meeting with the host, had a small reception, and the host will describe the menu. Then he proceeded to come into the kitchen with me and started cooking for the first course, making the dish beautiful in front of the guests. This was all in the hotel, but in reality, in the show, the scene was his house. We explained each course as they were served, and that was it. We ended the show with a glass of wine. Everybody was happy with the dinner. This was a great experience for me.

Every week the show "At the Chef's Table" had a different chef with an accent on a different cuisine, Southern, Italian, French. I think it aired in 2004.

Five Star Success:
St. Regis Monarch Beach Resort

*F*inally it was time to go. I didn't fully realize the huge task that was in front of me. Besides taking care of the five restaurants and large banquet facility, the priority was to regain the fifth star that the resort lost in 2005 and be able to keep them for many years. Just to be back at home with my wife gave me the courage to face my responsibility and what was expected from me.

The huge challenge to regain the star was launched. Everything needed to be upgraded, reviewed, fixed, changed, from the welcome to the service and the food. We started with a very extensive training program with Mobile and AAA. The undercover shopper from Mobile came around November and no one knew exactly when. He checked in during the day, then he or she had a meal at the pool, a dinner at the gourmet restaurant, and a late bite in room dining. The next day he or she ordered breakfast in room service, then a lunch in the bistro. He or she spent some time in the spa and had service there.

A few weeks later, we got the result of the inspection in a long, detailed report presented to the entire management team. A score is attributed to each department. In order to regain the star, the final score needs to be at 93 or better. It is very easy to lose points and that can happen very fast.

I didn't want my department to be blamed for not getting back the star. During the presentation of the quality and presentation of the food by the inspector, I prayed for a good result. In the end, my score was 94.5!

My department made it. The final score then was 93.7 for the entire resort. Congratulations to all managers, all our efforts and hard work paid off; we regained the fifth star for 2007! What a joy, and the best of all is that the resort kept its five-star and five-diamond rating until my departure in 2015.

It was very tough to maintain that status, specifically in the summer season. With transient business, the expectation is very high, and the hotel was at 90 % occupancy. Every restaurant was at full capacity, and the wedding season was at its highest, with an average of four weddings every weekend. I worked long, long hours, six or seven days a week. Nevertheless, we managed to do it. It took dedication and a lot of sacrifice. Within the first 18 months after I started, the resort was doing fantastically well, with an increase of 30 % of revenue. High-end group business was on the rise. Large groups of 400 people were the average, spending about $375 in food and beverage daily. Meeting planners were very exigent and specific on what they wanted for their groups in terms of food, ethnicity, quality, presentation, and action from the chefs in front of their guests.

Weddings were another large source of revenue. Many of them were Indian, Persian, and Chinese. In order to accommodate them, I created a large variety of menus touching every part of the world. Another very popular place in the resort was our wine cellar where I served a multi-course dinner with wine pairing for a group of up to thirty-five, in a private dining room surrounded by wine bottles and barrels. This, for me, was like being in an amusement park. I had carte blanche to create whatever I liked, from cavia, foie gras, and game to lobster, exotic fish, and much more. A huge training session with all sous-chefs and cooks took place, introducing new products, spices, cooking techniques, and presentations that considered seasons and costs. I was amazed to see the entire culinary team come together to learn and work hard toward the end result. This was a huge reward for me.

At the same time, I was getting recognized for my contribution to the hotel's culinary program. I even had a guest appearance on the *Real*

Housewives of Orange County, a segment in which the producers put subtitles on screen whenever I spoke because my French accent was so thick.

One program I was most proud of was in coordination with European and Mexican culinary schools to bring young cooks to the resort, who recently graduated, in good standing for a period of 18 months. This included about five cooks a year. For them, it was a dream come true. We spent many hours training them, and their collective performance was great. It led to an exchange in which our culinary team learned from them and they learned from us. Many of those students remained in the US on different visas and are now executive chefs in other hotels. This was my professional goal: to share and transfer my savoir faire to young cooks. This is also what it's all about to be a maitre cuisinier.

Another big program I had to do was "the passover" for a group of over 1000 people. They were very specific in their requests. Of course, everything had to be strictly kosher. For this, I went to New York to learn about Jewish cooking. It meant totally new training for me to learn the process, including what we'd need equipment-wise and the purchase of a completely new china. Even an article in a New York newspaper came out describing the huge luxury passover event taking place at the St. Regis Monarch Resort, mentioning the $15,000 per cost person for the ten-day event, the plan for how it would be organized, and the training of all the chefs.

It took six months to prepare. We drew up a menu for every single day, with five different meals a day. Then we had to prepare gourmet dishes for people willing to pay more money, so I had to create a menu for that. And all this had to be kosher. Passover is even more kosher than regular kosher. Some stuff you're not even allowed to buy. Two months beforehand, a rabbi came to visit the kitchen and told us what we could do and what we couldn't do. It meant a huge amount of organization and preparation.

The only part of an animal I could use was the front end, and fish with their scales on, dairy, and meat cannot be mixed. You have to cook in a separate kitchen specifically prepared for dairy or meat or vegetables with separate equipment. There were Jewish holidays where I couldn't cook with a flame, so all the cooking needed to be done the day before. They had difficult rules, which made it more challenging to cook five meals a day for a thousand people for 10 days in a row. I needed to provide a full dairy menu for every day, along with a meat and fish menu for guests to choose which they'd like to eat on that particular day.

Menus changed every day, and for those undecided about what to eat, a 24/7 tea room was available with a variety of salads, sandwiches, quinoa sushi, pastry, and bakery items. In order to serve that group successfully, my team went from eighty cooks to about one hundred and twenty-five, working ten-hour shifts that spanned an entire day. Even then, we could not always cover the demand. We were supervised by 20 rabbis, and everyone needed to follow the strict rules imposed by the Jewish passover law.

This was another great and successful experience in my career.

I have done a lot of big events, but the one that stands at the top took place in 2014. It was a wedding, which I will call the wedding of the century. With five hundred people in attendance, the weekend party lasted three days.

The final cost was seven million dollars!

It took one year to organize that wedding. I provided four tastings to the bride and her mother every three months, from ten in the morning 'till six at night, tasting food for different venues and different days, coming up with totally new ideas each time, and changing things.

The mother was demanding and difficult to work with, so difficult that she didn't fully trust me. She told me that I would be supervised by Wolfgang Puck for the main dinner. That was fine with me. I felt confident, and besides, Wolgang was a friend dating back to 1974 when he arrived in California to launch his career at Ma Maison.

The schedule for the entire event went as follows. For Friday, an informal lunch, and for that evening, an outdoor carnival with ferries wheel and other carnival amusements, plus booths and finger foods. Entertainment included headliners such as Stevie Wonder and others.

The next day, Saturday, consisted of another lunch with barbecue chefs cooking outdoors for the guests. The main event took place that same evening at the porte cochere of the hotel. The bride's mother covered the entire floor outside with a white carpet that was about 6000 square feet and added ten all-white grand pianos and 10 white violins. All the musicians wore white long tail tuxedos and played for the reception hour.

There were, in addition, twelve large reception buffets, some of them with standby chefs serving mini tacos, sushi, cheese fondue like raclette, and carving smoked salmon and pata negra ham from Spain. A large caviar station was also available with blinis cooked right there. The bride's mother spent over two hundred thousand dollars for an ice carving at every buffet. Ten-feet-high-by-40-feet-long ice curtains hung from a metal rod, separating some stations. Many ice balls were served with ice cocktails. (It was insane to see all that ice melting so fast.)

The entire hotel was decorated with white roses only. On the Thursday before the wedding, two semi-trucks unloaded white roses from different parts of the US. Once the reception concluded, guests were invited to the ballroom for dinner. Along the way, servers offered Cristal Roederer champagne, which sells for upwards of $300 a bottle.

I was blown away to see all the chinaware, silver, and glassware that had been rented for the dinner. Altogether it came in wooden boxes, individually wrapped in cloth. The plates looked as if taken directly from the period of the Renaissance, very elegant with gold rims. A crew of twelve unpacked and hand washed each piece from the entire set designed for five courses, enough for 500 people. It was very intense labor.

Once the entire room was set with those gigantic white rose arrangements and candelabras, it looked like a king was getting married. The entire dinner was plated in a minute with the help of 70 cooks.

I wasn't permitted a single error. Each plate was delicately presented hot and clean and paired with Stonish wine from Bordeaux and Burgundy. Château d'Yquem was poured for dessert. Everyone was very happy. The bride's mother personally thanked me for a great event. Then the guests moved to a different ballroom to enjoy music and dancing. More finger food was made for later in the night, with a wine bar and cocktails prepared by 2 mixologists.

There was a huge champagne brunch on Sunday, outside on a big lawn with Spanish live music. Chefs prepared all sorts of food, including a seafood paella, to honor the newly wed couple, as they were going to Spain for their honeymoon.

My stress level was so high over that entire week that, when everyone was checked out, I felt a huge release. Now it was time to focus on the next important event scheduled to start that same evening: the Allstate Insurance group arriving for their annual convention and awards ceremony. They booked the resort to serve as their headquarters, numbering about 350 people, from the CEO to the VPs and the best company agents. The rest of the group, about 2000 people, were staying in surrounding hotels.

I didn't really have time to rest after the wedding was over as Allstate had already scheduled their event, including a welcome reception, followed by a four-course dinner in a huge house in the hills of Laguna Beach, 12 miles from the resort.

I had only three hours to get ready and pack a truck with all the food for the 6:30 reception at the house. I was sweating bullets because the time was going faster than I would like. The truck got stuck in traffic and arrived about 15 minutes before the first guest arrived. This is when I really needed to keep calm and focused.

Thanks to God again, the event was a total success.

But this was just the beginning of another huge challenge. The group wanted to have their plated awards dinner for 2500 attendees at the hotel. The only possible way to do this would be under a tent on the golf course.

The timing was even more challenging. The four-course dinner could not last more than one hour and 15 minutes, max. The tight schedule already had attendees bused to the hotel at 5:45 p.m.; then dinner started at 6:15 and ended by 7:30. Then the entire group would walk to an adjacent tent, shaped as a theater, to be part of the awards ceremony followed by entertainment provided by the Aerosmith rock group.

By city ordinance, there can be no loud noise after 10:00 p.m.

The timing was strict and very tight. For this all to work, we set up one kitchen on both extremities of the tent, with six lines in each to dish up the dinner, with about 200 plates and five cooks per line. That's where I realized that good teamwork with great leadership is the only way to succeed.

Life under Pressure

*E*ven though I've had many successes, it is very difficult to please everyone, especially in the field of luxury. Expectations are high, and excuses are rarely accepted.

On the first consultation for the aforementioned century wedding, for example, the bride's mother made clear that she wanted to have the entire hotel available strictly for the event, with no disturbance of any kind. However, within the year before, our sales department booked the Allstate group function, representing over $1.5 million in revenue. For the Allstate affair to be ready with tents and stages, construction had to start 10 days prior to the event. So when the mother arrived at the hotel and saw huge tents going up, with a crane and big truck right in front where the wedding was to take place, she threw a fit. She screamed at my GM, yelling insanely, to the point where she demanded that Starwood corporate remove him in time for the wedding. She forced the hotel to pay for six fully grown trees, thirty feet high, to be planted beforehand in order to camouflage those tents.

During all that time at the St. Regis Monarch Beach resort, I felt great, happy for what I was doing. It was my cup of tea. My guiding principles were: Be attentive to details. Be constantly challenged. Stay on the high end of the industry.

But my time came to an end when the resort got sold to another management company. I left in April of 2015 and soon missed it.

Still, it gave me a rare chance to look back on what some of the tradeoffs are in this profession. For example, family life. It is very difficult for a chef who is passionate about performing at a high level to balance the work with the needs of a family. A chef's responsibilities include working long hours, holidays and weekends. It's not conducive to a healthy family life. My kids and my wife suffered from loneliness. Deep in myself I also suffered, unable to be at home to help with the kids' homework, unable to attend sports events at school, or even to share holiday meals together.

I never really could do what was expected of a dad or only did it rarely. My kids really missed out. They didn't have their dad's support, and my wife even more. She had to be both mother and father. Throughout our kids' youth, our time together was sporadic. The same with vacations—whenever I had one, school was in session, so we couldn't go out. Summers were busy for me. I had to work. So the only time we could take vacations was in January. So it was a hardship for the family. There were times when the marriage was very much in jeopardy.

I was warned about all the inconveniences of being a chef, but I ignored them for the love of the profession. The passion I had for it made me go on.

The toughest part of it was, when I decided to open the restaurant in France, I put my family through all that mess. This was a huge turn in my personal life. I spent twenty hours a day getting that place up, and then, after a little more than a year, I lost everything. For my wife it was very difficult; she lost her sense of security, for herself and that of the kids. At the time, it was very important for a woman to have security in a marriage. Our relationship suffered. When we wound up losing the business, the house, the cars, everything we owned, and our jobs, leaving us with just three hundred dollars in our pocket, we were forced to relocate with our two kids to a country where I didn't even speak the language. That really puts you to the test.

It was the lowest moment of my life.

Yes, the marriage suffered. But I always like to think that things will get better. I believe and trust in God. That's what helped me survive those tough times. There was a point where I went away from church and God. I became lost. But my strong roots helped me stand up instead of falling down and giving up.

It became a time of reflection for me. I kept working, but that day in church made me realize how much I missed my wife and kids. I laid everything down on the floor and asked, "What am I doing?" By then we'd been separated for nearly a month. It was a difficult time for me, her too. She felt terrible. I'd left her because she was so mad at me, going back to the time where we lost everything. I couldn't endure it. I couldn't handle it. It was my fault—I know. She was angry and couldn't forgive what I did. She became cold. She criticized everything I did. She wouldn't speak to me.

That day when I went to church became a turning point. I would go back to pick up the kids to spend some time together once in a while, whenever I could. On one of those days, I asked her to forgive me for what I did. I really wished with all my heart to come home. I'd try my best to be a better man, better husband, and a better father. It was difficult for her to take me back. It took a few weeks. The day she accepted, I had to put a lot of effort into fixing it and to show her I really wanted to be together. The scars were very deep for my wife, but with the grace of God, I did the best I could.

It took a lot of time. It still isn't what it was before all that happened in Nice. We went through many peaks and valleys and still do. We've come a long way.

It takes a lot of sacrifice and effort to make it happen. Not to give up when things become very difficult, and to make every effort necessary to have a better balance for the sake of my family, is hard to achieve. I could have moved out and kept going the way I always did, but no, I focused on family. I kept working harder and harder to make up what was lost. Many times, my dad came to mind. He'd sacrificed and worked so hard for my sister and me. This gave me the courage to keep going. Yes, I worked sixty or seventy hours a week. Yes, the road was rocky. But I realized my dream. We survived, and slowly, we climbed the hills again.

When you look around the world of being a chef, unfortunately there's a lot of divorced people. It's rare to see a chef who has stayed married from the beginning of his career. Most of the chefs I talk to are separated, divorced, or remarried two or three times. I put my wife to the test many times. She withstood the conditions, and for the grace of God, she continued to support me.

She's very smart. There are many times when she gave me good advice and I didn't take it. My ego got in the way. As a woman, she looks farther than a man, I would say. She has good judgment. Many times, after she's been right about something, I realize it later.

One example is the house we bought twenty years ago. I was originally looking to buy in San Clemente, but she gave a lot of reasons not to do it. In the meantime, she looked and looked until one day she found a house in Laguna Niguel. It was kind of beat up but with a lot of potential. I fixed it, and it turned out to be a good buy. It had a good location and a view. She was very to-the-point. I went with her decision, and it turned out well.

I want to point all this out because people get a false picture of what it is to be a chef. They think you become a movie star. But it's a difficult profession. There's so much to deal with. There's not just the cooking part. There's being a leader, a manager, a controller, a planner. Everybody depends on the chef for so many things. It's like what it must be to be a magician. People expect the impossible, and yet the chef needs to provide. And in order for the magic to happen, the chef needs to be surrounded by a great team.

Memories of a mentor in and out of the kitchen

CRITIC'S NOTEBOOK

Frederic Castan offers imposing talent, presence.

By BRAD A. JOHNSON
RESTAURANT CRITIC

The French chef who inspired me to start cooking and eventually open a restaurant – eons ago in Austin, Texas – now lives and works in Orange County. Chef Frederic Castan spent much of the past decade, unbeknownst to me, as executive chef of the St. Regis Monarch Beach. I learned this in August when a news release alerted me that he was packing his knives and moving to Hilton Anaheim.

Castan and I worked together at the Stephen F. Austin hotel, which was easily the poshest hotel in Austin in the '80s. He was the skinny but fearsome head chef with a heavy French accent. I was the skinny, naive, tuxedo-clad headwaiter. Chef didn't like waiters. We all trembled when he spoke.

The hotel's Remington Room was far and away the most expensive restaurant in town. Much of Castan's menu required last-minute flourishes at the table, and I was the one responsible for the tableside spectacle. If a customer didn't like the food, it was my fault. I cooked with fear until Castan taught me to be fearless.

Castan taught me to make the perfect Caesar salad. To this day, that salad is the standard by which I judge all others. Rarely does anything else come close.

Castan taught me to cook steak au poivre and to carve a rack of lamb. He intro-

CHALLENGE RODDIE
Frederic Castan is Hilton Anaheim's executive chef.

duced me to steak tartare. He showed me how to flambé cherries jubilee and crepes Suzette. I sent flames all the way to the ceiling, always putting on a good show. Night after night, I fried bacon at the table and turned the drippings into a spectacular dressing for wilted spinach leaves. I served Madonna and Cyndi Lauper. Customers rarely complained.

One night while I was flambéing a steak, I looked up and saw an irate, slightly deranged customer leap from his chair and rush into the kitchen. I knew I needed to stop him, but I couldn't because I had just lit fire to a skillet at a table on the opposite end of the dining room. I heard yelling from the hallway.

Within seconds, the customer came running back to the dining room even more quickly than he rushed into the kitchen. The Frenchman was giving chase, waving a large knife in the air, yelling "Get out of my kitchen!" Chef then scolded me for letting the customer get past and warned me to never let it happen again. I stuck to that bargain.

Alas, we were a passionate but ragtag band of pirates on

a sinking ship. The economy spiraled into recession, and the Stephen F. Austin went bankrupt. We lost our jobs with only two days notice. I never saw Castan after that. We hardly knew each other. He split town, and I eventually opened a restaurant with a few partners. We served his Caesar, which was our biggest seller.

This all happened so long ago that Castan says he doesn't really remember me. The news release touting his accomplishments doesn't mention the Stephen F. Austin, a place and time that clearly impacted me far more immensely than it did him.

Many times over the years, people have asked me how I got into this profession. I have often credited Frederic Castan as a key person in my life who put me on the path that inspired me to open a restaurant and eventually to become a critic.

Castan debuted his new menus in October at the Hilton's Mix Restaurant and Lounge. I stopped by for a taste.

I was surprised to find baby kale mixed into the Caesar's romaine lettuce, and the dressing isn't as lemony or as garlicky as the recipe he drilled into me so many years ago.

It's delicious, I guess. But it doesn't provide the déjà vu for which I was hoping.

Meanwhile, I can't help but wonder whether Castan still strikes fear in waiters. I hope so. The hapless waiter who served me could certainly benefit from a stern berating from the chef. Sometimes it's these moments in life that can open our eyes and lead us to something we never expected.

The Hilton Effect: Hilton Anaheim

When I started at the Hilton Anaheim in July of 2015, there was a lot of restructuring that needed to be done in the kitchen, and for me that required a huge adjustment. I had come from a luxury resort to a convention hotel. The food costs were way up there. I had to dig for a big cleanup.

By November, I had saved the hotel a lot of money just on food costs. I changed menus and trained new cooks. It was not easy. The union was not ready for changes. That was another obstacle in my work. I had to adapt myself and basically go with the flow. Fortunately, the management understood my vision and the need for changes. And they did appreciate that I saved them over seventy thousand dollars the first year on the food cost alone.

Since the big source of revenue at the Hilton came from banquets, I focused mainly on changing menus, following the trend, and cost savings. I then changed all the buffet presentations. That was a huge undertaking. During my second year, I spent a lot of time developing the concept of the chef's table.

To explain: There were once five restaurants at this facility. Four of them closed down. So they used the remaining space in the kitchen to make a nice chef's table. We created a special new design, including a wine rack on the wall. Guests became part of the action, watching the chefs cook. It's considered a privilege to come to the kitchen and be part of it.

The chef's table took off pretty well. This was a great tool for our site visit, to impress meeting planners, and of course to sign contracts for future groups. Often when a large group comes to the hotel, the meeting planner will treat the CEO and VPs to a nice dinner at the chef's table, with a wine pairing.

For me, I felt like a little kid in a playground at the park. If you're looking for a quiet place for a meeting, it won't be here of course. But at night, it's more for fun. I compare it to a movie set. When I see a movie, I am always intrigued by how it's done and seeing movie stars in action. I always compare a chef's kitchen with a movie set. Behind the scenes, you want to see how things come together. The noise, the yelling of the director, is part of it. It's all a show within a show.

The same thing takes place in a kitchen. People are intrigued by how dishes are created, prepared, and finished. They want to see the final touch before a dish ends up on your table. The noise is part of the ambiance, too, the rattling of the pots and pans, the loud voice of the chef, and the brouhaha of the servers.

In time, the chef's table grew famous, so much so that it became the color front page of the *Food and Beverage Magazine*.

I put one hundred percent into promoting this venue, from the selection of menus and wine, to training cooks and sales managers to make sure everyone was on the same page in being professional and understanding quality and the fine-dining experience.

There are 1600 rooms here. It's easy to lose stuff. But, of course, it's different from the other jobs I've had in my career. I've never worked in a big box like this before. But when you have a banquet of a thousand, it is much harder to do more refined work.

It's quite a bit different. With room service, some days are busier than others. We do between one hundred and twenty and twenty to one hundred and fifty covers a night. Combined with the restaurant, both can be three hundred, easily. Plus, we have the lounge and the bar and people asking for food there. Whether it's chicken wings or pizza, people like to munch on something. We have a nice charcuterie board where three or four people can have something to bite on. All this comes from the same kitchen. We do breakfasts and buffets, six or seven hundred a day, so we're very busy.

A big team of forty-five people came overnight for cleanup. They do the restaurant and banquets. Plus, having about one thousand employees here, we need to feed four hundred and fifty associates for lunch or dinner on any given day.

To cook for those people is another big thing to think about. We have a downstairs room that seats about eighty. They can have sandwiches, and there's a salad bar with eight to ten items. We have soft drinks and coffee; sometimes we do desserts. We have two hot entrees, plus soup, every day. We have chicken pasta that's served all day and tortillas with melted cheese.

If you want to have a free snack at three o'clock in the afternoon, you can go down and have chips and a hot sauce. The more you give, the more they complain.

"We had this last week."

Sometimes I'm tempted to say, "If you don't like it, why don't you bring your own?"

This hotel isn't booked completely by visitors to Disneyland. I'd say it's fifty-fifty. On weekends, there are a tremendous number of tourists. There are large bookings for holidays, especially around Christmas and Thanksgiving, when it's ninety per cent tourists. Summer is about seventy percent tourist. The rest of the year is groups. Insurance, technology, teachers, people here for sports events—a lot of it is tied to the convention center, which is next door. It's not just here.

When you have three or four thousand people for one purpose, that creates a lot of demand for hotel space. You have a convention center overflow. Not everybody pays for their meals. For a day or a day and a half, they're on their own. That's why we'll get a lot of business at the restaurant. After meeting until four o'clock, they all run here. We can serve up to two or three hundred people an hour. So the restaurant is difficult to manage. We never know what's going to happen.

The biggest obstacle I face working here [at the Anaheim Hilton] is dealing with the union employees. There are always issues. If I hire someone who I think is a good cook and is new and wants to work, I can't give him more hours than the seniors who have been here twenty or thirty years and may be lousy cooks. I have to give preference to those people first, and sometimes a good guy doesn't get any hours during a week, because there isn't enough work. I wind up losing good people.

The other handicap is that sometimes you have a very low turnover, which is great, but when you've got a team member that's been here twenty-five or thirty years, it's difficult to make them change. Then you wind up having to do a lot of work yourself. Another difficulty is that it's harder to maintain quality when you have to put out food in large quantities. It's not the same when you prepare two or three hundred and two or three thousand. That's another handicap.

I spend a lot of time watching the details of recipes. I take pictures of how meals will be presented. I make the dishes also, and yet, when I go back a few days or a week later, it's completely changed. Why? I don't know. Then I'll ask, "Why did you do that?" And I'll hear, "Because the people prefer it that way." If you can come here and eat something great instead of something average, why not? If you can have a good experience dining here, why not go for that?" Instead of thinking, "Who cares?" I've always put myself into what I cook, throughout my career. I've always put myself in the shoes of my guests, even if it's a hamburger. If you pay twenty dollars for a hamburger, you expect a good burger. So when you look at a burger you're preparing for a guest, you've got to say to yourself, "Did I give it a hundred per cent, or did I give fifty per cent?" Sometimes you come on the line where the plates are lined up, and you can see where the burger or the steaks are way overcooked on one side and way undercooked on the other. That's no good. It has to be evenly cooked. I can see it. But then I said, "Did you see that? You don't see anything wrong?"

I run this kitchen as if it were mine. I have to think about the bottom line and profitability and guest satisfaction. I have to think about health issues and running the kitchen safely, whether there's a wet floor or someone is using the wrong knife for the wrong thing. All this is important to me. I know what we need to charge because we're not a five star hotel. I need to adapt. Instead of lobster and caviar, I'll buy shrimp and something else at a cheaper cost. Nevertheless, it has to be quality. I'm not going to buy garbage. I look for prices related to what we're going to sell. All those things are my responsibility.

So far, it's been good. We make money. People are happy. I haven't diminished the quality of what's been here.

I'm thinking I'll stay two more years. It's always been in my mind to have my own place. If I'm financially okay, I'd like to open a little place for breakfast, from seven to two o'clock in the afternoon. It would range from breakfast to a light lunch. I don't want to work anymore than that. I'd like to keep a hand in cooking and the business. I've been doing this since I was twelve. I know I'd miss it. But it takes money. Maybe I could go into a partnership with someone and open just a few days a week. But when you do that, it becomes a job. You've got to pay the bills and this and that.

Is it worth it? I don't know. But I'd like to have something to enjoy.

And now?

What is for me in the future? What will I become? How will I accept the changes in my life?

In time we'll see.

ACKNOWLEDGMENTS

I am thanking God for the talent he gave me, for allowing me to be his instruments and enabling me to exercise it, to please and help others. And also for giving me a beautiful family, my health to be able to achieve what I did and keep doing.

My grand mother and my mom, watching the love they poured into each dishes, showed me the importance of cooking with passion

Claudia Schou, a good friend from the Hilton marketing team, thank you to push me to write this book, and all your time you spend structure it, understand my passion. Without you, it would not be a book

Maria, aka Cuca, for all your patience, trust and support during all those 48 years to be together .You are a wonderful mother and a very talented Artist painter, therefore I am dedicating this book to you for all your love you have giving to me.

One day, both of my son Georges and Brian, my grand children Aiden and Gianna, will read this book .I want them to know how proud I am to be their father and grandfather, and what an inspiration it is to have them as my children and grand children

To my parents, for their sacrifices, the education and Catholic roots they gave me, their everlasting love and support

I am so thankful to my dear parish St Timothy catholic church, for the spiritual guidance of Monsignor John Urell and Pastor Patrick Moises .

For all the support I received from my brothers Knight of Columbus and to use my talent involving all charity works .

My mentor chef Andre Chaussy (that later he became my brother in law), at the head of the Hielly Lucullus restaurant, a 2 stars in the Michelin guide, he taught me the discipline and respect of this profession. Thank you for pushing me to become who I am now.

To many other chefs that I cross paths with, long or short time, and who shared with me their vision, such as Paul Bocuse, Joel Robuchon, Pierre Gagnaire, and many others .

Azmin Ghahreman, a chef with a big heart, he rescued me a few time, and was there when I really needed.

To all the young chefs who have worked in my kitchens , who have given their dedication , energy and willingness to learn . To all the trainees , sous chefs, cooks, externs, stagiaires, who have worked as part of my brigade , I am so thankful for your loyalty and commitment . It is very rewarding to see many of you who have gone on to create your own success somewhere in the word. It is an immense joy as a chef , mentor knowing I have had some small influence on your career . You make me proud and remind me who I am in the first place . All members of the MCF and ACF , that form a large family , they all are very dear to me.

THE END

POSTSCRIPT

*J*une of 2020 marked my 52nd year in the culinary world, a profession I have always enjoyed and still have a passion for. I've accomplished many goals over those years. One of them was to become an executive chef in a luxury resort. Another one was to get La Toque d'Argent (Silver Toque) and Chef of the Year recognition among the best chefs in the world. All those goals did not come without sacrifice, perseverance, trust, and hope. But with our Lord's wisdom and guidance, He brought me to the top.

I never thought my career would end so quickly, but in March of 2020, without any warning, the Covid-19 virus invaded the world and made a huge negative impact on our industry; I was forced to cut short my career. I know that I will miss the opportunity to cook, to create, to be surrounded by professionals, and to be at the center of the action. I'll miss it a lot.

But I need to accept it and start another chapter. I want to dedicate more time to my children and grandchildren, to be more involved in charity work, and to help my church and my dear brothers, the Knights of Columbus. I also need to share my talents with young cooks, to encourage them in that beautiful rewarding profession of a cook/chef.

One big dream I never realized was to have my own little restaurant/ cafe with a small patio and exercise my specialty, making my customers happy in reflecting my native Provence and recreating some of my grandmother's dishes, which I'd like to leave to my children as a legacy.